"The ruins of memory lay untouched year after year. Covered by event upon event, these ruins refused to die. The breath of life was in them. Right deep down to the bottom layer. . . .

"You have decided to come and join me by digging through these ruins, to search and to find the reason for their breath of life and their right to live.

"Then, let us use our discoveries from among those ruins."

JOHANNA RUTH DOBSCHINER

"For me, her book was a light reflection from the many whom I passed in the years 1940-1945 and never saw again."

CORRIE TEN BOOM, author of *The Hiding Place* and *Tramp for the Lord*

SELECTED TO LIVE

Johanna Ruth Dobschiner

Pillar Books New York

Unless otherwise identified, all Scripture quotations in this volume are from the King James Version of the Bible.

Scripture quotations identified as PHILLIPS are from The New Testament in Modern English translated by J.B. Phillips, copyright, J.B. Phillips, 1958. Used by permission of the Macmillan Company.

Selected To Live was first published in England in 1969 by Pickering & Inglis, Ltd. This edition is edited for the American reader.

SELECTED TO LIVE

A PILLAR BOOK
Published by arrangement with Fleming H. Revell Company

Pillar Books edition published December 1975

ISBN: 0-89129-036-2

Library of Congress Catalog Card Number: 73-8780

Printed in the United States of America

PILLAR BOOKS is a division of Pyramid Communications, Inc.
919 Third Avenue, New York, New York 10022, U.S.A.

TO

all my good friends throughout the United States of America, especially to those in Pennsylvania and South Dakota whose lives and prayers enabled me to serve our Master in your country.

FOREWORD

> I read . . . all the good wishes of the host of people all over the country whom I will probably never see again. I've kept their wishes, their photographs, their love and their prayers and will always remember them. To them I owe my life, my health, my soundness of mind, my hope when, at times, all seemed lost.
>
> In memory I salute them all—men, women and children—from up in the north to the low south, each one did their part to create within me a truly thankful heart.

That is what Johanna-Ruth Dobschiner wrote in this book. She was one of the many for whom the Lord used us underground workers of Holland to save their lives during World War II.

This book describes the suffering of one of the many persecuted Jews, but the blessing of this book is that Johanna experienced and saw the miracle of Romans 8:36-39—that in the life of a child of God, nothing can separate us from the ocean of God's love in Jesus Christ.

A completed Jew, she knew her Messiah Jesus, who has promised: ". . . lo, I am with you alway, even unto the end of the world" (Matthew 28:20). For me, her book was a light reflection from the many whom I passed in the years 1940-1945 and never saw again.

God bless the reading of this book.

CORRIE TEN BOOM

INTRODUCTION

The ruins of memory lay untouched year after year. Covered by event upon event, these ruins refused to die. The breath of life was in them. Right deep down to the bottom layer.

The ruins of memory breathed and sighed and were part, and always will be part of the modern, new society; they will be part of this present day with its joys and sorrows; they will be part of the approaching tomorrow with its events still veiled and hidden.

The ruins of memory begged to be always part of life. To be, to remain, to belong, to be treasured, to be acknowledged, to live forever!

But why do they want to be part of the present? Why not remain covered by hawthorn, holly and spring blossom?

Because I live and always will live. Within me are those countless millions whose souls will never die; who lived, loved, hoped, feared, and trembled like myself . . . for myself and my own kith and kin. Their bodies were worth nothing, their blood as cheap as water, their feelings and pain but smoke and ashes.

You have decided to come and join me by digging through these ruins, to search and to find the reason for their breath of life and their right to live.

Then, let us use our discoveries from among those ruins.

JOHANNA-RUTH DOBSCHINER

SELECTED TO LIVE

CHAPTER 1

Adolf Hitler's birthday was a great event. It was April, 1933, and all schools were invited to take part in the great parade. Our school brought its own token of respect and gratitude to such a leader.

We had planned and prepared a gift since autumn of the previous year. The senior boys had made a large frame and in it was placed a picture of the Fuhrer. The picture was full of little holes like a pegboard. We were asked to bring three pfennigs to school for one nail, black, white or red. Indeed, we were encouraged to bring many pfennigs to school, for it was fun to hammer nails into this picture pegboard, to see it taking shape, until, finally, a full-color portrait of the Fuhrer had been completed. All the money would go to the party as our contribution for all the Fuhrer was doing for the Fatherland and—the world!

Primary and senior classes assembled in the gymnasium. Each class was headed by a flagbearer. As their names rang out over the loudspeaker system, joyful "ohs" and "ahs" could be heard here and there; my six-year-old heart felt like bursting when I heard mine. I had been chosen to lead my class!

Coming to the Reichstag, we met the Fuhrer. All

right hands were stretched high with a fervent shout of "Heil Hitler." He greeted us with his "Heil" and a broad smile. The portrait was handed over by the senior boys and the procession moved on. Bands and music surrounded us for hours.

Conversation that night dwelt mainly around the events of the day. Fancy, our only daughter, chosen to carry that flag! The committee couldn't have known who she was. Or had the decision been influenced by evil intentions? We would never know.

Our home and shop were situated in the Ullstein House, the property of a large newspaper and printing firm. Beside the shop was a huge archway with two high, double-glass doors. Going through them you found yourself in a marble hallway from which you could reach the various floors and departments. We, however, walked across the marble hallway and through another swing door to the backyard. Passing through yet another hallway the dwelling houses could be reached.

We children loved to play in this spacious labyrinth of passages. Although we were happy children we were all older than our years. Responsibility was ours as far back as I can remember. We were not to air our opinions regarding the new reign in the country, not to mix with Gentiles apart from school hours and not to repeat home conversations. The innocent chatter of a child had already brought imprisonment and death to many a parent. Even teachers at school could be trusted no longer. They were compelled to question their pupils regarding the home attitudes toward the Fuhrer and his party.

We were still under the protection of the Dutch government and its consul in Berlin, but which rascal or hooligan would possibly know that we were Dutch Jews! All over the city, shop windows of Jewish properties were smashed, and slogans painted on walls and dwelling houses. It could be our turn next.

A new era dawned during 1933. Family ties grew stronger and relationships between in-laws strengthened. We saw more of each other and appreciated the worth of family and friends. There was such a gap in age between my brothers and me. Werner was six years older than I was. His twin, a girl, had died on August 30, when only three months old. I was born on August 30 six years later. Just a substitute, according to his boyish teasing, but a treasured gift in the eyes of my parents.

Werner was a fair boy. Taller and thinner than Manfred in outward appearance, he also seemed more fragile, yet his strength was respected on the playground at school and also at sports. In nature, both boys were very similar. They were good friends, had many interests in common and were home loving and quiet. Chess or checkers were a regular weekend activity in our home. During the better weather we could always be found in the park. The boys liked these walks and joined us as often as possible.

Manfred was a year younger, darker in appearance and, if anything, quieter than Werner. When Werner, always technically-minded, wanted to have fun and experiment, Manfred withdrew to his music and study. Music was born into the very fiber of his boyish nature. He could pick up any instrument and play the tune of his choice. At twelve years old, when taking part in his first concert at high school, the program read "Manfred, the wonder boy."

Many were the offers which came our way regarding educational grants for a future career in music. The reply was firm and always the same, "Our son must learn a trade; he shall work with his hands. Knowledge in his fingertips will see him through any crisis he may have to face in his future life."

Weekends, the boys spent their time together, showing interest in each other's hobbies and talents, or joining in experiments. The electric train set always needed to be modernized and often it absorbed them till late on Sunday night.

I loved to play outside. The park and lots of children were my delight—the freedom, fresh air, sunshine and laughter. There were long avenues and many hilly stretches. In winter we took our sleds and the fun was tremendous. There were ducks and swans; any stale bread or crusts were confiscated for them. My father took me to this paradise whenever time would permit. He was a wonderful man whom I respected, loved and admired.

My mother was one year older than my father. There was little she could not do. If we wanted something, she could always help. If she didn't have the time to do it immediately we could rest assured that she would attend to the request at a later date.

I am glad I was born and I am glad to recall my childhood. I treasure the memory of home and family life. I am grateful for the strict training and discipline that were mine during those early years. I am puzzled and bewildered by the experience which war and deprivation pressed on us all, but I have learned that a loving invisible hand held mine through it all and I am firmly convinced that neither death nor life, nor angels, nor principalities, nor things present, nor things to come, will be able to separate me from the love of God, which is revealed in Christ Jesus.

CHAPTER 2

Although anti-Semitism in Germany was on the increase, our home and family life were still relatively safe, our Dutch nationality the only security. Repeatedly, the Dutch consul in Berlin informed my father that he could not continue to be responsible for our safety. Youthful enthusiasts did not inquire about their target's nationality. Already, at high school, my brothers had been molested. Headmasters no longer had any control. Party politics roared through schoolrooms and colleges.

The Dutch consul advised early emigration to Holland to begin life anew in my father's hometown of Amsterdam. The next few months were a succession of events. The business, which had been in our family since 1884, had to be wound up. All goods were sold off cheaply as time was short. The furniture left in a large van and soon our flat was empty. A taxi took us from home, the only one I had ever known, to the station, the gateway to an unknown future for us all.

On the platform we met all our relatives and their children. It was an emotional reunion and farewell. I, however, was too young to understand the anguish of such a moment. To me, adventure and the unknown future beckoned with excitement and thrill. I was looking forward to the journey and the new country ahead!

Late in the evening of April 10, 1935, we arrived in Amsterdam. Here we were, in our own country, but none of us could speak a word of Dutch! Since we had no relatives or friends to meet us, we awaited the arrival of a Jewish community representative, feeling more like refugees than Dutch citizens.

After what seemed like an eternity a Jewish-looking gentleman approached us, and, in broken German, discussed our immediate future with our parents. Then he packed us all into a taxi, which took us to the Asylum for the Homeless.

We showed our papers to the watchman at the wooden gatehouse, after which the community representative left us. The watchman led us to a barely furnished dining hall, where an attendant seated us on hard wooden benches, before a long table covered by a wax cloth. Soon we were luxuriating in the warmth of steaming mugs of tea, served with white bread and jam.

My father and brothers were taken to the male section, while Mother and I were led to a large bathroom. The nurse showed me where Mother would wash, then she washed and dried me, and thoroughly inspected my hair. In a very short time, a clean but tired and humiliated little girl joined her mother at two beds set in the center row of an already dimmed dormitory. Mother reassured me that the men would be all right, and in a short time we fell asleep.

At breakfast next morning, everything seemed much brighter. We were able to laugh and joke about our experience of the previous night and compare this dining room with that depicted in *Oliver Twist*. We all agreed it must have been the same, the only difference being that we were offered a second helping!

That day we set out to see something of Amsterdam and to find the Jewish community buildings and its offices. In a fortnight it would be the annual celebration of the Jewish Passover, and we wanted to have a solid roof over our heads for this feast with its intricate ceremonies and special food laws.

During our wanderings we ate snacks of herring, cucumbers and onions from the favorite Dutch herring barrows, and drank cups of lemon tea in street cafes. Although we were free from persecution, we were strangers in our own land, but we were content and thankful. Soon a settled homelife would unite the family again.

Rented houses could be found, but were they within our means? Father was out of work, my brothers still had to find a trade and be accepted as apprentices. I had to go to school. The Jewish Board of Guardians and Assistance came to our aid, and visits to the National Assistance Board and the Labor Exchange became daily routine.

After some months the lease for our first home was signed. The house in a nice bright street in the east end of Amsterdam near a lovely park, the Zuider Zee and the open-air swimming pool. All houses in this district were comparatively new council flats, each building housing four families.

An interesting feature intrigued us: at the top of the building there was a flat of attic rooms. Each tenant owned one of the rooms as a storage place. Outside of each front attic window was a strong iron bar with a hook at the end. All houses and factories had one. It was a clever device to help with furniture removals. Nothing was carried up the stairs; all articles were hooked in the van and pulled up to the flat in question.

As soon as we became settled in our new home, my brothers were apprenticed to local businessmen—Manfred to an optician. Werner to a tailor. And I was enrolled in the airy and bright local school.

My first days were strange indeed, a class full of Dutch-speaking children and a Dutch teacher, with me unable to speak a word of the language! Yet, it was not long before I was able to chat and joke in Dutch, along with the other children. Games in the large playground at school, and after-school games on the street in front of our house, contributed a great deal. And, after several trips to the open-air swimming pool with our teachers, I, too, learned to swim and was very proud of my prowess.

On Friday afternoons, we Jewish children were excused early in order to prepare ourselves for our Saturday Sabbath. Even my brothers came home early from work. The whole family participated in this preparation, for every detail was important: the silver polishing, setting of table, shopping, preparing of meals. This breaking of bread and drinking of the blessed wine has always been the most impressive act of worship in the Jewish home. Each member of the family partook of these elements in strict rotation, from Father to Mother and then to each child. Once this act of worship was performed, my father placed his hands on each of our heads and blessed each of us children individually. For the boys, he asked the Almighty to bless them and let them grow in wisdom like Abraham, Isaac and Jacob; for me, to become like Sarah and Rachel and to be fruitful and multiply.

On Sunday mornings and twice during the week after school hours, I went to Jewish classes in order to continue my religious education. I loved every minute of these and was first in all subjects. The rabbis always regretted the fact that I wasn't a boy! The lessons seemed to come easier to me than to most of my classmates. Ours was a good orthodox home. The example there was the best teacher in the subjects others had to be taught from a book. I read and wrote Hebrew fluently, knew my prayers by heart and could recite sections to be said only by boys, for I heard them each morning during prayers at home. These quiet times were observed strictly by my father and brothers alike, as soon as each was washed and dressed and before they came to breakfast.

On Saturday mornings we went to the small local synagogue. Saturday is the finest day in my memory. Warmth, love, unity and holiness was the theme pervading and uniting us all. I treasure this day and all the Jewish festivals. The weekdays with their strain and worry could be set aside and forgotten. At the weekend we were refreshed to face another week and all that was in store.

My father was still looking for a steady job. The stumbling blocks were age and language problems. Having left Holland at the age of four, few accepted him as a Dutchman and just smiled at his treasured passport. Often he had temporary jobs as a representative, but that would not keep our heads above water. Mother accepted piecework, and we all helped with the finishing touches of her stacks of wallets. As a matter of course, my brothers handed their weekly wages to my parents, who in turn gave them a small amount of pocket money.

Once a year we received a special voucher from the National Assistance Board. Then my mother took me to the Central Corporation Clothing Department, where I was fitted with a red and black checked woollen dress, brown woollen stockings, black shoes with a clasp, white flannel underwear and a navy blue rain cape made of smooth felt. They were new and warm and I loved them, but it must have hurt my parents to allow me to be clothed by the State, when in Germany only the finest quality and styles were good enough for me!

Yet how could we complain, when such sad and worrying news reached us from relatives left behind in Germany? The same news reached us from my father's relatives in Poland. Cries of help from all directions. We were free, but not at liberty to invite others into the country. We would have to be responsible for their maintenance, and this we could not do. Father's brother Jacob had been thrown into Buchenwald Concentration Camp, and his wife and children pleaded with us to do all in our power to get him out and over to England.

How and what happened is not known to me, but Queen Wilhelmina was, in some way, instrumental in getting him out of Buchenwald and into Britain. All traces of his wife and children were lost and as far as we know they did not survive those years. Now he lives, or rather exists, a stunned, broken, sad and disheartened human being, his mind dwelling upon the past.

Other cries for help came from my father's sisters in Poland. What could we do for his aged mother? Surely we could not stand by idly and see her in danger in her ripe old age? No, we could not, even though it meant a major reorganization of our homelife.

Soon after we moved into a larger flat a short distance from our first home, Grandma arrived. She was extremely emaciated and in poor health. We loved her, nursed her, spoiled her. My father was a most devoted son. It was a treat to see my father and grandmother together, but their reunion was not to last long. She died two months after her eighty-second birthday, three months after entering our home. She slept peacefully away in her son's arms, but in a free country, buried with dignity and respect on free soil and in a Jewish cemetery.

Once more our homelife fell into a regular routine allowing us to enjoy two normal years. I emphasize *normal* years—so strange and yet so true. In this period I passed through the last year of primary and the first year of secondary school, the only true study I have ever known, although I remember practically nothing about it today. Yet they were normal years to me, with normal events and normal friends.

My parents booked a holiday to help me forget the stress and strain of the past years and the death of my grandmother. They thought it important that I should meet and have fun with children of my own age and religion.

At the end of a dark green tree-lined avenue, on the top of a hill, was Hilversum's Children's Home, a large white building surrounded by lovely grounds. There were fields for games and adventure corners for the younger children. The tiny tots had all they could wish for, sandpit, swings, chute, etc. My favorite game was football. I cherished the boys' title for me, their "best goalkeeper" of the season. These were very happy weeks. There, my desire to become a nurse was born; there, the true spirit of friendship was born, the value of the true team spirit and the love for many people. There, I met the nurse who was to become my heroine during a difficult period in my life. There, I matured and became more self-reliant and independent.

Pleading letters from relatives reached us almost daily. What could we do? They were not Dutch and the government could not accept immigrants in great numbers unless their resident relatives would guarantee their full financial support.

In sure desperation, some members of Mother's family left everything they owned to book passage on an immigrant ship for Havana, Cuba. Along with their fellow passengers, they withstood seasickness and depression, in order to establish a new, free life. Their city of refuge gleamed in the bright sunlight, when the blow fell—with no explanation. Cuba refused to allow the captain to enter the harbor! Radio messages explaining the shortages of food, the desperate plight of the passengers who faced certain death if they were returned, were to no avail. Some passengers leaped into the sea, but were quickly recovered to continue a seemingly endless voyage.

The captain tried several ports, but none would permit this shipload of Jews to enter. Finally, France, Belgium, Holland and Britain each decided to take a share of this odd cargo—only those, however, who had relatives in that particular country.

Our seven relatives were interned in the Lloyd Hotel in Amsterdam—a seaman's hostel that had been hastily cleared and prepared for them. Here, they were able to eat, sleep—yes, even relax—until the government located homes for them. The Jewish community helped out by contributing furniture and household necessities.

CHAPTER 3

On the morning of May 10, 1940, I awoke contentedly to what I thought were familiar sounds—the beating of carpets and blankets. Everyone knows the cleanliness of the Dutch housewife: her wash flutters in the morning breeze long before her family arises; her neighbors join together to whang away at their already immaculate blankets and carpets.

Then I heard voices—fearful and loud. I sprang from my bed and tore wide the curtains, as all of my neighbors were doing, and saw the sky dotted with black objects. As my eyes strained, I realized they were men—men dangling from parachutes!

A few fell like fragments of dust, hit by our machine-gun fire, but most descended unharmed. An army of German soldiers had invaded our country—quite literally out of the blue!

No one went to school or office that day. We clustered together, hoping against hope. The fighting was fierce; the Dutch soldiers fought with real courage, but to no avail. By nightfall, German soldiers were everywhere.

Having escaped the claws of the advancing bear for five years, we knew ourselves to be in a trap. From now on, every day had its own unpleasant surprises. New rules and regulations were to be found almost daily in the headlines of press and radio. Most of these were directed toward Dutch Jewry. Jewish people had to hand over their bicycles, cars, radios, etc. In industry, Jewish businessmen had to leave the work to their Gentile partners. Posters outside shops stated bluntly to close their doors to us.

A wave of anti-Semitism swept across Holland. When Dutch citizens refused to obey, they found themselves treated as Jews. We were forbidden to use public transport of any description. Jewish children, having been compelled by new regulations to leave their present form of education, were placed in an entirely Jewish day school. It was a long walk each day for my friends and myself, in all kinds of weather. Sometimes I wonder if this enforced exercise and the strange schooling did depress us children. I cannot recall; we were as happy and contented as we could be, learning day by day to become as wise as serpents and as harmless as doves.

The winter of 1940-41 seemed wetter and colder than previous years, and my parents decided it was time to move once more—now, and for all time, to the Jewish quarter of the city. Here we could enter shops freely. Here we were near the synagogue, the school, friends and a Jewish doctor.

After our move the first decision made was that I must leave school and learn a trade, in order to equip myself for whatever life held in store. Becoming a tailoress—what could be more dull and boring? It was absurd; it could not be *my* life—sorting materials, sewing endless seams, delivering orders to the rich and not-so-rich!

I hated every day of it, but somehow I learned. And it was a real thrill to turn over my wage packet each Friday, just like Werner and Manfred—especially when half a dollar was returned to me for my own proud pocket money!

It was a special treat to deliver a garment I had helped to make; it broke up the monotony of the day and, if the delivery were in the late afternoon, I was allowed to go straight home. There was one old house, facing a canal, that held a special charm for me—the brass door handles always shone; the tea-table silver always gleamed; the maid who admitted me always smiled; and the lady of the house always tipped me generously!

On those treasured days when I made late deliveries, I headed straight for the large Jewish hospital on the Northwest Keizersgracht. Here, I could loiter in front of the main entrance and sniff the hospital smells and watch those much-envied uniformed girls, veiled sisters and white-coated doctors.

I wanted so badly to become a nurse! One weekend, I spent my pocket money on a bottle of methylated spirits—how a sniff of that bottle encouraged my drooping spirits to stick to the goal! Gradually, I acquired several medical instruments, and fitted out a first-aid box; I kept all these treasures in a black leather case, which I treasure to this day.

My parents would not hear of my training to be a nurse, so it was only natural that I turned to Sister Henny, who had befriended me on my glorious holiday at Hilversum's Children's Home. She had achieved her life-long ambition and was now a nurse at a large hospital. In her off-duty hours, she encouraged me to ask questions; she also knew how to put me in my place!

Was it any wonder I turned to her whenever I was frightened or perplexed?

CHAPTER 4

The rumor of yet another new law and regulation became reality overnight—all Jews were compelled to purchase bright yellow stars, five inches in diameter, outlined in black and inscribed with the word JEW in capital letters. These stars had to be sewn firmly on outdoor clothing, dresses and suits. No Jew was allowed to leave his or her home without this notable insignia on the left breast pocket.

Now we were outlawed indeed—seen and known of all men, especially by those who sought to destroy us. Day by day, as it had happened years ago in Germany, people disappeared mysteriously. Round-the-clock arrests were the order of the day. Those who had means and connections often found an underground hiding place. It was risky and a big step to take. Once you had taken this course, you had to stay underground, and remain illegal till the war ended—favorably!

Whole families disappeared by other means They wanted to keep the Honor to themselves, not wishing to face the future of slow, but certain, extermination. The gas taps were the easiest way out. It did not frighten the children.

Suffering draws people together. Father's brother, a

widower, and his young teen-age daughters wrote from Belgium asking if they could come to stay with us until things blew over in Belgium. There, too, the iron grip of the enemy had tightened and daily life had become more burdensome. My parents' reply, of course was, "Come over as soon as you can," and early in February of 1941, Uncle Michael, Edith and Ruth arrived in Amsterdam.

Saturday, February 21, 1941, was a pleasant day, yet still cold. A brisk walk after dinner would do us all a world of good, my father suggested. Would I show the girls a little piece of Amsterdam's historic beauty? But I had a previous arrangement with my girl friend, Rita, from the orphanage around the corner. So my brothers obligingly offered to take the girls around Amsterdam.

I walked to the corner with my parents and uncle, where we went our separate ways—they to visit the local rabbi, I to meet Rita. "See you later," were the words that followed me.

Rita was waiting for me in the hall, and we embarked on our usual expedition, looking at the windows of the city stores. Happily, we admired the new spring fashions for the teen-ager. Gradually, we became conscious of gloomy and frightened looks around us. Some people started to run. We overheard snippets of conversation which aroused our curiosity even more At last someone bothered to answer our questions. Their reply made me go cold and stiff inside. "They are pulling up the bridges and are going to raid the whole city center."

Screams of frightened women were mingled with the brutal shouts of soldiers. Little children, perplexed by the sudden panic, ran from their homes and wandered whimpering along the streets. Suddenly, there on the other side of the bridge, we saw the cause of the terrorized atmosphere. Dozens of Gestapo had pounced from their lorries on men and boys within reach. All who wore the yellow star were seized and pulled in one direction. The manhandling was terrible to witness. We were frightened and started to run as well. We ran and ran until were were out of sight of those helpless victims.

Even here, the atmosphere had been affected by the human explosion across the bridges. The streets were empty, except for a few, like us, who were looking for refuge.

We were shocked; our voices sounded shaky. Where could we go? Neither of us knew. Walking steadily away from the troubled area, we came to the Weesperplein. The people here seemed unaware of what was happening across the bridge. Seeing the J.I., I remembered that the matron of this home for elderly Jewish people was my own dear former matron of the children's home in Hilversum. We could go there.

She was not in, but the porter allowed us to wait in her sitting room. It seemed like eternity, but at last my dear matron arrived. I began to cry and Rita joined in. Matron's hand rested on my shoulder for a moment, then she proceeded to make tea, leaving us to cry. It relieved us a little and on her return with the tray, I was ready with the question, "Can we stay with you, at least until the soldiers have left again."

Matron assured us that we were welcome to stay in the home as long as we needed its safety. At 6 P.M., after another session of tea, sandwiches and fruit, Matron suggested we try to make our way home. She had made inquiries, and it seemed all clear again. We thanked her, but left hesitantly and with heavy hearts. Never again would we be the lighthearted youngsters we had been prior to this incident.

That fifteen-minute walk home was an eerie and nauseating experience. The streets remained quiet and forsaken, but from houses along the route, sobbing, shouting and hysterical anguish reached our ears.

Crossing the bridge over our canal, we parted company. Rita went back to the orphanage and I walked along the water's edge toward our house. I could see my cousins on the steps in front of the flat. Their red, swollen faces, their wet eyes, their sobbing told me enough. "Where are the boys?" I demanded. "Where are Werner and Manfred?"

Sobbing heavily they told me what I had suspected all along: the boys had been arrested during a demand for eight thousand men between the ages of eighteen and forty. They had been dragged away from Edith and Ruth, pushed and kicked toward the Jonas Daniel Meyer Plein. There, the thousands of men were herded together, made to kneel down on the bare cobbled stones, raise their hands high above their heads and remain in that position until the order was withdrawn.

We unlocked the front door and wearily climbed the stairs to our flat. The fire in the stove was still warm and bright. Yet I shivered and couldn't stop. Edith and Ruth quickly produced three tumblers of Russian tea. With both hands around my tumbler, I tried hard to think straight. It was unbelievable. My brothers gone! Where would they be taken? Would they be allowed home again?

The voices of my cousins roused me from my frightened thoughts. How would we tell my parents when they returned home? Would Father be all right? In deadly silence we stayed together, waiting, thinking and drinking tea.

Within the hour my father ran into the flat. "Where are the boys?" "Where are the boys?" he shouted again, his eyes staring at us fearfully. Meanwhile, my mother was grief stricken. My uncle stood beside her, trying to comfort her a little, and assuring her we would find out whatever we could before the night curfew. My cousins were sobbing again, and my father, completely beside himself, paced up and down the living room repeating again and again, "Oh, the boys, the boys, the poor boys, oh, Werner, Manfred, ah, the poor, poor boys."

I was still dry-eyed and completely stunned by all that had happened and also somewhat frightened by all the commotion. Uncle Michael was the only one in control of himself. No one slept much that night. We heard shouts outside and the revving of car engines. All knew what this meant—more arrests! Our thoughts were with our boys. What had they endured already, what lay before them? Would they be warm enough? Flogged? Starved? How long could they stand it?

Weeks of waiting and worrying passed before we received official notification that Werner had been sent at once to a labor camp. Buchenwald, that dreaded and familiar place that had ruined Uncle Jacob, was once more connected with our family! Manfred was supposed to be at Malthausen.

My parents were distraught. "Our boys are separated," they cried. "Now they have nothing to hold on to, lost among a host of men of all types, ages and backgrounds."

Our homelife changed drastically. My uncle and the girls found a flat of their own, and the three of us remained silent for the most part, talking only when we picked up one of the many rumors that drifted through the city. There was no real direct news from the camp; any news that did leak through, by illegal means, was so fearful we tried hard not to believe it.

More arrests occurred daily, and we mutually decided that the struggle for survival was on—we would endeavor to keep alive, even if it meant separation. We would try to stay together as long as we could, but we must be prepared. Each of us acquired a rucksack and filled it with bare essentials and official papers, some tinned food and toilet accessories. With marking ink, name, address and date of birth were written across each. Soon, most Jewish people had such bundles in the halls of their homes. Everyone was prepared!

Three months after the arrest of my brothers, word reached us that Uncle Michael, Edith and Ruth had been arrested overnight and were on their way to the unknown. Once more we could do nothing. We were helpless in the claws of the invader.

My parents grew more quiet and more despondent. Then came the fateful day we received official notice to forward a stated amount of money to cover packing and postage of Werner's ashes and his few personal belongings! Kind, gentle Werner had not been able to withstand the rigors of Buchenwald. Secretly I was glad—Werner was too young to have lived forever in the semi-world Uncle Jacob inhabited. When we received them, we had our doubts about the ashes, but we accepted them and buried them respectfully.

As the months went by and we had no news of Manfred, I grew more and more concerned about my parents. I hated to leave them alone all day long, while I sewed away at the Ding-Dong's for a meager wage. I turned many ideas over in my mind, but one kept returning. There were so many orphaned children in the city, and we had an empty room. . . . Why couldn't I mother some of these pitiful waifs, and bring life into my parent's grieving existence?

I tried to talk to my parents about the idea, but their one glimmer of hope was that Manfred might return; they refused to even consider the idea. Finally, the dread word came—Manfred too was dead. Now, we had truly lost our boys.

After much discussion, my parents agreed to contact the Board of Guardians about taking in some youngsters. They inspected our flat, and soon sent two extra beds, so we were able to foster four children!

First came Susan and Mirli, aged twelve and nine; then Hermann, who was ten; and last but not least, Margaret, who was three, and spoiled by all of us—parents and older "brothers and sisters."

It took a while for the children to settle in, but they knew about our boys, and it was a link that helped make us into a new family. We had no blood ties, only ties of race, circumstance and deep personal loss

When my parents agreed to accept the children, they had insisted I continue tailoring while the children were in school. But one day my patience came to an abrupt end, and I just walked out! It was not until I was halfway home that I realized the full consequences of my impetuosity—the loss of my weekly income. Abruptly, I switched course and made for the hospital and Sister Henny.

When I left Sister Henny at the hospital gate an hour and a half later, I was wiser and more mature. One more step had been taken in the school of life. *Consider other people's feelings, consider others!*

"Hansie," Sister Henny had said, "you want to be a

nurse when you grow up. You want to care for people and help them. You can hardly wait for the day when you are old enough to put on a uniform and be called a nurse. If you want to be a real nurse you can begin to train right now. Go home, look at your parents, look at them, long and deep, think about them and realize that they are broken and sick. Their own flesh and blood has been torn from them. Boys they have loved and cared for throughout childhood and youth, through illness and problems of adolescence—their pride, their hope, their boys have been taken from them suddenly. Try to realize the pain and suffering they have endured, the agony of mind and loneliness and the utter finality of death. Hansie, don't be hurt if your parents seem unfair and unreasonable to you. Dismiss all seeming unfairness, forget it, train to be a nurse—now! Go home, be a good and kind nurse to those two broken people. Tell them you've come home to be with them, to help with the children. At the same time, get a job near home, just a few hours morning and afternoon, to bridge the financial gap. Go home, Hansie! Be a nurse!"

It was the usual time when I entered the house. I could choose the time to drop the bomb, time to brace myself for the inevitable explosion. After dinner I ventured to explain. I was bombarded by a burst of words from both Father and Mother. I tried to be understanding and calm—I so wanted to be a nurse. I did not even cry when the silence of the night at last came to our home. The ordeal was over. No more tailoring for me. I was free!

News travels fast, and I soon heard that the local schoolteacher and his wife wanted a young girl to take care of their two small sons while they were at work. No time was to be lost. The very next day I called at the house, a few minutes distance from our own. I was welcomed by a very nice young couple.

My love and desire to look after those small boys was uppermost. The parents sensed this and asked when I could come. The next day was the earliest and I remember that I rang the bell long before the agreed time. The whole care and feeding of the little ones, the choice of clothing for each day, when to visit the barber, when to go for a walk, all these were to be my responsibility. Each day I passed my home with them, collecting my mother's shopping list on the way. The boys grew to love her and she looked forward to this daily break from housekeeping and strain.

These were wonderful weeks and months. Knowing oneself to be needed and loved gave such an added zest to life. It made one grow inwardly, resulting in outward contentment, joy and happiness This, passed on to others, in turn brought happiness.

With the falling of autumn leaves, many people around our neighborhood disappeared mysteriously. Like those who had gone before, they were never heard of again. Whole families were seen no more. We all knew where they had gone, but no one spoke the word *underground*.

The Dutch Resistance Movement was very active, and their around-the-clock-watch-and-work can never be overestimated. Much is known but very much more can never be known, for these heroes died in helping the persecuted.

Everyone wanted the chance to go underground, but not everyone could afford such safety. It was an expensive business to live for months, perhaps years, separated from society, family and friends—to live and depend for your life and safety on the love and kindness of fellow human beings, who endangered their lives by saving yours.

My first encounter with this situation took place one morning in the summer of 1942, when I rang the bell of the house where I cared for my little ones. There was no answer, and, at first, I did not know whether it was arrest or underground. The neighbors soon informed me that no raid had taken place during the night. So, it had to be the underground.

Out of a job once more, we all decided it would be best for me to stay at home and help my parents and the children; we could manage on the meager stipend the Board gave us for them.

Daily, more people disappeared. Jewish minds worked overtime, trying to assess situations as they came up; often innocent-seeming incidents proved to be cleverly designed preludes to mass deportation. One learned to listen for the stopping of heavy lorries, opening of car doors, rough voices—day and night. Those who were lucky went underground to live in attics, cellars or secret cupboards of thousands of Dutch well-wishers.

I knew that the hospital staff and patients lived in comparative safety, but my parents still refused to allow me to go into training, so I decided I would endeavor to become a patient!

I made my way to the big hospital at the Nieuwe Keizersgracht in Amsterdam, and Sister Henny. "But my dear," she insisted over and over again, "we can't admit you if there is nothing wrong with you. It would endanger the lives of Matron and all of us if it were known that a fraud was in our midst." I pleaded that she should use all possible influence to take me in before the curfew that night. Reluctantly she told me to be at the main gate at 7:45 P.M. precisely.

The day continued normally enough. It was Friday and Mother prepared the dinner of the week. We always had lots of extras on Friday nights and a lovely homely atmosphere into the bargain. I could not refuse any food during dinner in case my parents would suspect anything. Then, during tea, I told them of my plan.

"Mother, Sister Henny is allowing me to sleep in the hospital tonight. Father, just in case they ring the bell tonight, tell them your daughter is very ill in the hospital and has to undergo an operation."

"Good gracious, child, have you lost your senses? We don't want to lose you as well," my father said. Mother added her objections, "You can't go to the hospital if you are fit and well. What are you up to?"

Quietly I interrupted: "I'll be all right, Father. I'll go to sleep there, and you sleep here at home, and we will have tricked the angel of death once more. Don't worry, Mother, I'll be all right." I collected my comb, towel and facecloth and left the house with a casual, "Cheerio, everybody, don't worry."

Success! They had not suspected the truth of the matter. I was on my way to the hospital: the play had begun.

At the appointed place Sister Henny was waiting for me. Accompanying her was a towering, broad-shouldered giant with bushy red hair. Although he was dressed in a doctor's white coat, I knew it was the radio control engineer. He would pull the strings and get me admitted illegally. I had burned my bridges, and could not turn back. It was 8 P.M.!

The next fifteen minutes passed as on a race track. I was hustled upstairs in a lift, thoroughly prepared for the operation to come, while Sister Henny for once talked nonstop. "Well, have you made up your mind? What would you like us to do? Amputate a toe, a finger, break your leg and set it? Make a scar and stitch it?" We discussed my anatomy in record time. The bargain was made—my appendix for a fortnight's safety!

One obstacle, however, could not be removed—the heavy dinner in my stomach. The risk had to be taken, we would commence with a local anaesthetic plus the extra-large incision for possible inspection purposes. But it did not work. Soon I became very breathless and restless and the surgeon ordered a general anaesthetic. Drifting happily over green fields, I spent the best part of an hour in absolute freedom without a care in the world.

It must have been well after midnight when I wakened in the ward. A kind, middle-aged nurse watched over and comforted me. I was so sore, and continual bouts of sickness ripped the pain in my wound. Mercifully that night had an end, and when morning light entered the ward, my stomach was truly empty and at peace—and so was I!

One ordeal was over and the next just around the corner—visiting hour at 3 P.M. There was my father. Cheerfully, he entered the ward and spotted me at once. As he sat down, his chair bumped against my bed, making me flinch just a little. Quickly, I covered my error by asking for Mother and the children. He chatted, lightheartedly, for less than three minutes, then told me to get ready as soon as possible as he wanted me to help him with some messages that afternoon. No one had called that night in our street, but shouting and screams had been heard from neighboring houses. No one knew when they would reach our door. Suspense, always suspense.

There was no easy way out. Plucking up what courage I still had left, I told him the truth. "Father, I've had my appendix removed. I can stay here for a fortnight. No more worries until then." At first he was speechless, then a torrent of words poured over me. Finally, he left me a bag of yellow plums and departed most unhappily.

My head spun like a top. I wanted to sleep, to be sick, to talk to someone nice, to drink, to do anything but just lie there. I felt, oh, so lonesome.

It seemed an eternity before Sister Henny came to see me that night. She nodded and smiled at me, stroked my head and held my hand. Her comfort was a heavenly balm to me.

Soon the ward settled down for the night. Nurses had performed their regular duties, dressings had been changed, medicines given, beds remade and the suppers served, when two Sisters entered the ward with another lady. They spoke to my night nurse, who was preparing herself to go on duty. She looked very upset when the two Sisters left, leaving the lady behind. The night nurse came over to me and explained that I had to be moved to another smaller ward. It had already been darkened for the night, but by the shimmer of the duty lamp I saw one window at the end of this narrow small ward. My bed was nearest the door and I noticed three more beds. A lady sat beside the duty lamp, but did not even come over to welcome us. The orderlies left me with a final "good luck," and after reviewing my new surroundings for a short while, I fell asleep. It had been a heavy day, physically as well as emotionally.

Very early next morning I received the foretaste of

yet another ordeal. I raised myself for a drink from my locker and that lady stood beside me! Where had she come from so suddenly? Looking at her pleasantly I smiled a good morning, but a short and sharp reply was all she managed to produce. I could not understand it. What was she doing here? Soon a nurse arrived with a bright, "Good morning, ladies." With her was another person who exchanged places with that stranger-of-the-night. The other patients had made no attempt to converse so far. Sheepishly, I glanced at them. It distressed me. They looked very depresseed and I assumed that their illnesses must be of a very serious nature. I was sorry for them. Little did I know that they were only meant to speak when absolutely necessary. While nurse served the breakfast, my curiosity reached its limit. I asked her about this strange ward with its exchange of ladies. Her information chilled me through and through. "You realize, my dear, that this is the official sickbay of The Theater. When you are better, you must go back again. The ladies are the official warders; they are responsible for you until you join the deportations once more. We are only permitted to nurse you."

My wound was forgotten; I sat right up. "Nurse, it's a mistake!" My voice rose steadily. "I've never been in The Theater. I did not come from there. Please get me out of here." I started to cry and the new lady came over to me. She was more kindly than her predecessor.

"Please lie down and do not cause any trouble for us. Do as you are told, and you will soon be out of here."

"Yes, I know," I interrupted her, "I will be out of here, but I don't belong to The Theater; I don't belong to The Theater, I've nothing to do with The Theater. I want to go home."

(Near my home, a large theater had been taken over by the occupying forces. After removing all seats and other furnishings, arrested people were herded together in this large hall, awaiting the dreadful moment of deportation. Evidently some people fell sick, developed complications, and were sent to this hospital to be nursed and guarded until they could resume their journey to the land of no-return.)

But where did I fit into this muddle? I had never been arrested. Or could my parents have been caught after all? Had they explained that I was here? Were they being allowed to remain at The Theater until I was able to join them? It could not be! Who would have predicted two days ago that my own arrest would take place in the very building where I had sought safety for us all?

By late afternoon I was beside myself. I hadn't stopped demanding the doctor, crying and protesting that a mistake had been made. If my parents had not been arrested, what would become of them if I were taken away! I had walked into this trap and plunged us all into misery! In near hysterics I rose from my bed, the stitches forgotten. I wanted to get out and away from here. The lady stood beside me once more. She literally saved me from a nasty fall. Exhausted, lightheaded and speechless, I was laid on my bed. Someone rang for the nurse. "My doctor, my doctor," was all I could demand at that stage. An injection did the rest. When I came round, my doctor stood smiling beside me. His hand on my shoulder, he spoke reassuringly: "Put your belongings on top of your bed, and we'll go back to where you belong!" Now I sobbed with joy and relief. A sharp twinge went through me, however, as I left my silent and sad fellow sufferers. I knew I would never see them again.

Within ten minutes I was back in my former ward. Word had spread about the mix-up in index cards. The strange and sudden manner of my admission had been mixed up with other strange and sudden admissions. Who had been responsible we would never know, but how I needed the following twelve days for recuperation in my ward, under the care of my doctor!

My arrival home was comparable to that of a fairy godmother. It was Mirli's birthday and I was able to present her, and all of the others, with lots of small luxuries, farewell gifts from my well-wishers in the ward—fruit and chocolates and raisins and half a bottle of orange juice. Before nightfall I would be able to finish the dress I had promised her.

That night I turned around in my bed with a heart full to overflowing. I would not listen tonight. Surely nothing would happen this particular night. "Please, let nothing happen this happy night of reunion," I prayed. "Let us all sleep without worry, just this once." We all did sleep that night and nothing happened.

Chapter 5

Next morning I awakened rather early and remained quietly under the blankets. Judging from the comparative silence in the flat and down below in the street, it was early yet.

After breakfast I helped the older children get ready for school. Soon the house was quiet and Mother made another cup of coffee which we drank silently together. Somehow, there was little talk between us these days. We just enjoyed the luxury of being together. I felt helpless to suggest any subject or to begin a worthwhile discussion. As always, actions had to speak louder and more directly than words.

Marijke, next door, knowing about our children, had given me her large and most loved doll. She looked very sad and thoughtful when she placed the doll in my arms. "Love her for me till we come back, will you?" she almost pleaded. Should I ask any questions? It was quite plain that they had received a call-up with the morning post. "Of course we'll treasure her," I assured Marijke. "Give my love to your parents . . . see you soon." It sounded casual, but then, we all knew what to expect. Any good wishes would sound artificial; it was better to say little than to sound insincere.

Often I wondered about our neighbors in the convent nearby. They seemed to live in a different world altogether. What did our life mean to them? They had to adhere to a routine. The deadly silence in the building after the sound of a gong was so contrary to the chatter and laughter in the backyard during their free time. They skipped and ran, played ball and told stories; they were happy and gay whenever I looked down. I was told they prayed a lot and for very long at times. Oh, well, everyone had to make his own choice.

Gradually the days closed in; the signs of autumn were all around us. The trees in the park across the canal were quite bare. Winter clothes came out sooner than in previous years. Winter gales arrived and with them colds, sore throats and flu. Not having had proper nourishment for a long time, our resistance was lowered more rapidly. Personally, I had never felt quite right since my operation. I'd felt washed out for weeks now. My eyes were burning and my throat felt so dry. It pained me more from day to day. One day I noticed a red glow all over my skin. Thumbing through my medical book, my heart leapt for joy. Could it be true? Scarlet Fever!

Not wishing to raise my parents' hopes too high, I did not mention my discovery. I told them only that I felt terribly ill and needed a doctor. They realized that I spoke the truth. The doctor called later that morning and changed the atmosphere in our home into triumphant joy: he confirmed that it was scarlet fever!

Six weeks of absolute freedom—no worries, no cares! We were compelled to attach a sign outside our door: "Danger. No entry, scarlet fever." This and this only would hold the invader at bay. Complete security, such bliss!

Our homelife developed a new routine. The children were prohibited from attending school, so each one was allotted a small duty in the running of our home. We had nothing to grumble about. We were safe behind closed doors as we prepared for a happy Channuka feast. This feast of dedication in the Jewish home is celebrated about the same time as Christmas. We, too, give presents, sing songs and burn candles. We celebrate the victory of the Jews after yet another battle, and the rededication of the Holy Temple, made possible after finding the famous cruisken of oil. Judas, the Maccabee, with his servant, searched frantically for oil to obey God's command to keep the altar light burning at all times. But everything had been destroyed; no oil could be found. Great joy echoed throughout the camp when just one drop was found. Wonderful, oh, wonderful, this one drop burned for eight days and nights, lasting until new oil could be brought to replenish the stock!

Since then, each year, for eight days' duration, this lovely feast of liberty, dedication and victory is celebrated. Each day, one more candle is lit, until on the eighth day eight candles plus the servant candle are brightly cheering all who recite the ceremonial blessings and thanksgivings. Songs are sung, presents distributed, fruits, nuts and sweets are there for the taking throughout the duration of the feast.

That year we celebrated with very grateful hearts, for we had each other, plus the safety of scarlet fever. We made presents for each other, such presents as were possible during these years of restriction and deprivation. Our gifts were practical, with the occasional luxury of some specially-baked delicacy.

Being still in bed, my thoughts traveled far and wide and my mind was acutely active. We were safe for the time being, but how long would we be able to stay together? It was a fact which had to be faced. How would we react to separation? I could not imagine my parents' lot, they were so dependent upon one another. And where would I finish up?

It was at this time that I became God-conscious for the first time in my life.

If one has been raised in a happy Jewish home, religious life is a joy and a tie which binds all members with cords of mutual trust and understanding. Traditional observances, burdensome to the eye of the outsider, are natural and full of delightful privileges to the Jewish family. We were orthodox and quite strict in the observance of our religion, and the synagogue services were never missed although we had to walk a great distance to get there. But—was Almighty God part of our everyday lives?

Suddenly it shook me deeply to realize that He was so badly ignored, never considered and mentioned at all except in prayers during private and public services. Was He a reality at all, or just a memory from the ancient days of our patriarchs? Was He interested in us or just a negative vague spirit? Could He, and would He, if called upon, hear and answer any requests? If He were real, if He could be contacted, and if He could hear. . . . But why did He seem so remote? Whose fault was it? He had been close enough to Moses and other great people in our history.

There, in that bedroom, a mighty truth penetrated my whole being. It was like a message from on high, a strange experience indeed. I was awed and full of joy and gratitude. The experience expressed itself in three words—GOD . . . WITH . . . US. These gave me strength, depth of life and a determination which had to last me for the next two years. Over and over I repeated them in thought, even whispering them aloud. In December, 1942, this remote person, the Almighty God, had allowed me a glimpse of Himself. . . . I now knew that He was and is and would come again. Three words now stood rock-like in my life—GOD . . . WITH . . . US!

Where had they come from so suddenly? It did not worry me. I felt rich and full and wanted just to bubble over and tell this great truth to all. But where to begin? Well, right there at home. Now or never, I had to share it with my parents. I had to tell them before it was too late. Once they knew it, too, they would be able to face the future with courage also, whatever it had in store.

I told the family not to disturb me as the Hanukkah presents still had to be finished. This was an easy way to be left alone and it was the truth. From this moment onward I worked constantly and very hard at the finest presents ever and the most practical, too.

But first the decoration of my room had to be finished. Since I had to stay in bed, the candles would be lit in my room and the evening would also be spent there. Three large sheets of writing paper were to carry my three words, decorating the wall above my bed. I drew the words with the loveliest, curliest letters I could possibly manufacture. A lovely border surrounded each word and all was colored in bright, blending shades. Admiring my handiwork, I pinned the paper in place.

Searching in my drawer, I picked the whitest handkerchiefs I could find. On each one I embroidered the words "God with us." While working and planning the evening, I thought deeply about what I could say to my people. No, what I had to say! Since that moment of revelation I was compelled to tell them about it. I could not and must not withhold this truth from anyone. It was a gift, and it had to be shared. As if I belonged to an invisible someone, I acted as under orders.

As usual, Mother had been preparing the meal all afternoon, planning to be free for the celebrations that night. Inwardly, I dreaded the moment when she would open my door to bring me the evening meal. But the unavoidable moment came and—"Hope you like your di . . . what is that? Did you make these?" Mother pointed to my display.

"Yes," I nodded, "do you like them?"

"Very nicely done," she replied. "How on earth did you think of it?"

I said that I would tell her later, hoping that some curiosity had been aroused. So far at least, I had been successful. All the same, she must have realized that something was brewing, because I heard broken sentences to that effect from the kitchen downstairs.

While the family continued with dinner and the clearing and washing of dishes, the newness of this revelation continued to burn itself into my being. GOD WITH US.

Soon it was time to begin the evening's festivities. The table was covered with a tastefully embroidered tablecloth. The freshly polished brass *menorah* (a candelabrum) was adorned with just one white candle and the servant candle, which would light the candles each day till at last eight candles would burn brightly on the eighth day. We were handed our prayer books and we turned to the section for Hanukkah. Father began by reciting the blessing, the thanksgiving, and then lit this one lonely candle with the *shammos,* the servant. Now the time had come to join in the singing of the *moautzur,* the song of Hanukkah—a beautiful song, a lovely melody, a memory and tradition many thousands of years old. A rich treasure was ours, to be part of God's people, the children of Israel.

Our eyes met, while singing this song of triumph, and my voice faltered. We all knew that our thoughts were the same. Oh, our boys, our poor boys. Why all this unnecessary suffering? Continuing the final verses of our triumph song in a weak voice I looked longingly at my God-given verse. "Oh, heavenly Father," my soul sighed, "please keep Your promise! Do not leave us, don't forsake us!"

The song was finished. We all shook hands and kissed one another with tears in our eyes. The children smiled shyly and we smiled through our tears.

Clearing my throat and taking a deep breath, I realized that the greatest moment of my life had come—to encourage my parents, because the Creator wished it so.

"Mother and Father, and you children, too, I want to speak to you and give you a few words which have come to me while lying in bed. We should not be sad or serious at Hanukkah, but we should face reality, not just celebrate the liberty of our forefathers. We, too, want to be glad. We want to find comfort and hope during our days of Hanukkah in this difficult year. There can be comfort and hope if we take Almighty God at His word. Mother and Father, we know what has happened so far, but we don't know what will happen in the days to come. We are still together, but we don't know if we will be in the near future. . . ."

"Don't talk such utter rubbish," my father interrupted.

Then Mother chimed in: "Let her talk, Leo, and afterwards I'll make the tea."

"Whatever happens," I continued, "and should we get separated, wherever we are, let us never forget that . . ." and I pointed to the words, "God with us." "He will be with each one of us, all the time, everywhere. Please don't let us ever forget it. It will be our strength and comfort until we meet again. That's all, I just wanted you all to know this and to remember it! Always! There is only a little present for each of you this year, but it will be the easier to keep it with you. Never forget its truth and its comfort."

It was all over. I handed them their presents, first my parents, then the children. They unwrapped them and looked quietly at the words. Each one said a quiet "thank you" and I felt very uncomfortable. Yet my mission was completed, and I hoped, very sincerely, that the words would have the same effect on them as they had had on me.

"You are only a child; you have no need to talk so depressingly. We are together and we will remain so." With this statement, my mother slammed the bedroom door and stepped toward the kitchen to make the tea. We were still quiet when she returned with the cups and saucers.

Reality had to be faced and as devout Jews it was high time to think of the promises of Almighty God and take Him at His word.

How He would be with us, I did not know, but *He* knew, and I believed!

Into early February we managed to maintain the smell of Dettol on our landing and to keep the sign "Danger, infectious disease" on show. Yet, these good days had, inevitably, to end one day. Braving the storm once more, life, returned to its usual cat-and-mouse game with the enemy in our midst. We felt that the Sword of Damocles really hung on a very thin thread and we lived quietly, solemnly, earnestly from day to day. We were extraordinarily kind and patient with one another. Did we unconsciously number our days? Had the Gestapo noticed the long duration of our danger notice? Had it made them alert to their neglect of Number 107 in that street? From March of 1943 onward, the dagger pointed unmistakably to its neglected prey.

One of the greatest heartbreaks was the general call-up of the pupils from the secondary schools. Boys and girls alike received these call-ups by early morning post. On a given date a week later, they had to assemble at midnight in the Central Station in Amsterdam. They were needed for "practical work" at some labor camp. Each had to take his rucksack and a blanket. Midnight—during the normal curfew hours—ensured that they had to come alone; no parents, no scenes—total separation at once. None of these children ever returned!

I still remember, today, the bitter cries of despair one could hear toward the midnight hour as parents opened their doors to let their children go.

One morning late in March, the Gestapo stood at our door. Inwardly shaking, we made haste to open. They gave us no time to think or imagine the reason for their visit. With calm assurance they made their request: they had come for ten-year-old Hermann. He, hearing his name, endeavored to make a quick getaway, but the soldiers grabbed him and left as suddenly as they had come. We were stunned and speechless. Was it not enough to have taken his parents and the other members of his family? Could they not have left this child in peace, to survive, and to grow up within our fairly secure family circle?

At 8 P.M. as curfew was about to begin, a loud banging on the front door shook us to the core. Yet, one always hastened to open at once. It was an inbred reflex action. The children stood as though rooted to the ground, Mother sat stunned at the table and Father was right behind me when I opened the door.

Our Hermann was home! "I got away, I got away!" was all he murmured over and over again. We did not ask him any questions, we just looked at his grin and were thankful to have him home again.

After such an eventful day we all slept soundly that night, only to awaken to an even more horrifying day.

They were back by 10 o'clock to look for their prey once more! That was the end of our little boy.

One morning, soon after the departure of Hermann, I returned from shopping to find the children in tears. Father and Mother had been collected and taken to The Theater for questioning; the rucksacks were gone. Fear gripped me. Was this it? Had the end come at last? The oldest girl, Susan, assured me that they would be home by nightfall.

I tried hard to think straight, then, putting Susan in charge, I told them I would soon be back. I had to go to The Theater to assess the situation. Just ten minutes from our house stood this building of terror. Would they allow me to see them? I ran all the way, arriving there breathless but determined. Heiner was my only hope—a distant relative of my father's, a person we never saw around the house—surely he would not refuse my earnest plea. In some way he worked for the enemy. Or did he? I could not understand the complicated situation, but I did not care, I wanted to free my parents and I had to use this means.

I approached the Gestapo on duty. "Sir, I wish to see my uncle, Herr Heiner. Please put me in touch with him." Not wishing to hear the answer in case it would be in the negative, I stepped back and gave my attention to an undone shoelace. Once this imaginary mishap was rectified, I rose and looked into the most kindly face I'd seen for a long, long time. Karl Heiner was a very sincere and helpful man. There was no need to tell him anything. He had seen my parents on arrival and had been in touch with the authorities on their behalf. I pleaded with him to make sure of their release. He took me into a little room and gave me solemn instructions. We were not to look excited or worried: it would endanger his and our position. He looked at me for a long time, then slowly and emphatically, he said: "Go home and get the dinner ready—they'll need it!" I shook his hand firmly and gratefully and walked with him past the guard. We parted with a smile to avoid betraying the real object of my visit.

This surely was an act of faith, for I *did* prepare the

dinner and set the table with the finest tablecloth and the Sabbath cutlery.

As promised, they arrived home by dinner time. What a reunion! We laughed and cried and remained very close together all that evening. Yet, I have never discovered just why they had been arrested. Was it meant as a foretaste of things to come? They had been greatly surprised to hear their name over the loudspeaker system that afternoon—to them their freedom was a miracle. They were upset and broken after the sudden arrest and we all took a sedative and went to bed before curfew. We would at least try to get some hours of sleep should the arrests be repeated. It turned out to be another sleepless night and then another bleak day faced us all. We all realized that safety was ebbing away. Only a miracle could keep us together.

I dared not mention my Hanukkah encouragement, so I only asked rather hesitantly if they had packed their handkerchiefs and their bookmarks. We did not shun reality any longer. Sitting together like condemned slaves, we discussed certain essentials. Father impressed on us that it had to be every man for himself and God for us all, and not to make the mistake of trying to stay together. If one was arrested that one must go and the rest seek safety, anywhere. We understood only too well; we sensed our days were numbered and inwardly we prepared for the parting. Father put our thoughts into words. We must be strong and accept a possible parting until the war is over! No one replied; a sense of depression descended on us and remained with us from that day on.

We addressed each other in terms of endearment and went out of our way to be kind toward each other, from morning till night. It was an altogether frightening and very unhealthy atmosphere. When would the incident of Hermann's rearrest repeat itself for us as a family? Every new day was a burden, every night a ghastly experience. We lay awake, listening for the heavy army lorries. Would they stop tonight, or pass on once more? When heavy army boots sounded on the pavement, we automatically held our breaths. Often we heard that determined hammering on someone's door. Whose? Oh, God, help us, send deliverance, somehow, from somewhere. Give us courage and strength. Be with us!

Every man for himself, my father had ordered. Could we do it? Would we, when the time came?

Drearily April made its entrance. The dismal gray weather was a true reflection of our attitude to each hour of our lives. Even the hands of the clock seemed to drag themselves wearily over their prescribed course. Was there no way out? No one to help? We kept our thoughts and fears to ourselves. Shopping, eating and sleeping became a mechanical exercise. The nights continued to be a nerve-wracking experience. It was good to meet over breakfast every morning; we treated it as a gift. We learned to look long at one another, desperately trying to imprint each other's features on our memory. A heavy sigh to Almighty God was heard frequently in these days. Our prayers had no words; our whole beings craved freedom and security.

CHAPTER 6

On the ninth day of April, 1943, at 10 P.M., our bell rang loud, long and continuously. We knew at once that this was it! My heart thumped! I buried my head in my pillow and burst into a flood of tears, sobbing and frantically beating my bed with my fist. No, Lord, no! Please, please let us stay! The children, in their bedroom next door, were disturbed by now. The heavy boots of the soldiers came nearer and nearer up the stairs. The children cried and called for me. Susie, the oldest, quieted them and warned them not to mention my name. They wouldn't stop and I couldn't either. I cried, tore my sheet and shook all over. Why did no miracle come our way? Now, this minute! Please, Lord, come and help! "God with us." I couldn't feel it now. I had told my parents to believe it and hold onto it. Oh, Mother! I could hear her crying with pain. Had they hit her? "Get out of that bed this minute or a bucket of water will bring you to your senses!" Father appeared to be trying to protect her and to calm the soldiers. I could hear him reasoning with them. Poor Father, he was a broken reed himself. Suddenly all was quiet. Was Mother dressing hurriedly, or had something horrible happened in that bedroom? Someone came upstairs.

"Come on, children, hurry!" It was Father. "Good girl, Susan, bring the children into the sitting room. Are you warmly dressed?" The little ones still cried for me. Then my door opened slowly and quietly. It was my father: *Bleib gesund mein Kind!"* (Keep well my child!) A quick kiss on my hot wet face, and he was gone.

Oh, no, the soldiers were on their way up. A hard voice said "Hurry up, everyone, we haven't got all night!" I kept perfectly still as I heard him moving about in the children's side of this large partitioned room. I expected the dividing door to be flung open at any moment. But at last, his footsteps faded away, as he went downstairs.

Mother's voice had regained its normal tone. She asked permission to see if the gas and electricity had been turned off at the main. Her quick steps came nearer, passed the kitchen, the switches and made for my door. I knew it, I knew she'd come. "Oh, Muttie." She embraced and kissed me warmly: *"Mein liebes Kind, bleib gesund, halt Mut!"* (My dear child, keep well, be courageous!)

They shouted for her. A last hug; she was gone. The door banged and I heard them all tramping down those wooden stairs, then the starting of the heavy engine as the lorry drove away from the house.

A ghostly silence enfolded the building. I dared not move, yet my brain worked at double speed. It was a frightful night. Listening to every sound, I wondered if the house would be looted before morning. It was still curfew time, but looters knew quite well where arrests had taken place, and the seals would not be applied until the next day. If they found me, would they notify the police? I'd heard of assaults and rape and the bribery of silence for consenting victims. Weak with shock and the realization of the danger of my position, I remained motionless for a long time.

When at last I was able to relax I knew I had to act quickly. This would be my last night in our home and I had to use the time wisely and well. In pitch darkness I dressed, putting on as many garments as possible. Every movement, every step, had to be watched to avoid the creaking of floorboards, stumbling over a shoe, knocking over a chair. Although my movements were as quiet as possible, my plans almost perfect, someone must have heard me when I used the toilet later on, for I heard heavy footsteps on the landing. They stopped outside our front door, and there was silence, as if someone was listening intently. Then followed knocking on the door, over and over again. I was petrified, but I was determined no one would get me to open that door. If they wanted me, they would have to break it down and find me. I stayed in the toilet till I heard the steps fading away.

Once the silence had returned, I planned the next few hours. My rucksack could not be taken from the house. That would be fatal. I would take some essentials from it and repack them into a very small case. Although I looked everywhere, however, no rucksack could be found. Had father hidden it to avoid suspicion? There was no time to think or worry about the matter. Replacements had to be found—toilet articles, some cutlery, an unbreakable cup, a change of underwear and a few sugar lumps, important papers, addresses, and writing material. This had to suffice as my little black case was full.

Fully dressed with hat and coat, and my little black case beside me, I spent the last night in my home. It was the longest night I have ever spent: it seemed as if six o'clock would never come. Silence, darkness and fear surrounded me. I said a mental farewell to all our belongings, knowing full well that I would never return.

I awoke from my daydream as dawn found its way through some small cracks in the blackout paper. It was close to 6 A.M. My head began to spin again, but I had to be strong. This was no time for sentiment. Clear thinking was of the utmost importance. No one must know that I had left for good. Once more I went through the rooms and silently bade a final farewell to all the memories they held for me.

The crucial moment had to be faced; very quietly I edged myself through our front door, trying to avoid the inevitable squeak if it were opened too wide. I did not want the neighbors to know that I had been left behind. If I had not been missed, I might be free a little longer. In time lay hope, hope for survival, hope for a future. Holding my breath, I raced down the two flights of stairs, realizing that practically every one of these wooden steps was certain to creak. At last I stood in the cool morning air and stepped out briskly, as if filled with a definite purpose and aim.

The streets were quiet. Here and there was a cyclist on his way to work, a milk lorry, a van returning from market and the inevitable fearsome green lorry, perhaps on its way off duty.

Only ten minutes from here was The Theater to which my people must have been taken. Opposite The Theater was the day nursery where I had just begun a new career a few days ago.

Hesitantly, yet deliberately, I reached the main door at last. Not daring to look across the road, my eyes fixed themselves on the bell, listening sharply for steps in the corridor. Yes, someone was coming. The bolt and lock rattled, then clicked; the assistant matron looked in amazement at my expressionless face. "You are early, my child, come in."

"They called last night . . . the whole family . . ." was all I needed to say. She did not even reply, but put her arm gently round my shoulders and led me to the office. After a short silence I had to ask the vital question: "Did you hear any trams last night?"

She nodded and left. The minutes and hours ticked by. The morning rush hour had begun. Cars and people, lorries and trams were speeding on their daily tasks. Was it an extra dull day? An air of misery seemed to hover around and over us all, or was it just over me? Cups of tea and coffee were handed to me from time to time, but my eyes would not leave those doors. Every move of officials and soldiers was weighed in my judgment. No one attempted words of comfort. Everyone knew why I was there and who had been arrested, and they left me in peace. All at once, something shook me from my state of semishock. The sudden revving and roaring of engines made everyone in the building take notice. What we saw turned many a face ashen pale. My blood ran cold; I was unable to utter a word. An extra transport had begun.

More than a dozen army lorries were lined up outside The Theater. A sorry stream of people left the building heavily laden with bundles and rucksacks. The children, who only a short time before had been fed by us, were now carried outside by their mothers, or a nurse who handed them to their fathers. Short, harsh orders intermingled with the despairing cries of the unfortunates. Helplessly, they disappeared into the steel-plated army lorries, up two steps and another broken heart and tear-stained face was on its way to. . . . I could see them no more, the windowless body of the trucks hid all its misery from view. As each one was filled to the brim, the living load was secured by the flap being lifted into place and the iron pegs clicked into their holes. As lorry after lorry moved off another empty one took its place. At last the flow diminished. Only two vehicles were left and they filled up rather slowly. Was this the end for today? Had I missed them, or had they been spared just a little longer? Where there is life there is certainly hope as well.

A gasp escaped me—there they were! Mother came first, white-faced but tidily dressed even after the ordeal of arrest and a night in The Theater. Hesitantly, still hoping for a miracle, I suppose, she struggled up the few steps into the army lorry. Directly behind her was Father. He was ashen-faced, his eyes stared without expression before him as if he did not care where he was going, and his very movements gave the appearance of a mechanical robot. In seconds, he, too, had disappeared. Mother turned her head toward the nursery. Had she hoped that our eyes would meet just once more? It was not to be. Barely a minute, and the heavy revving of the engine set the lorry in motion. It also brought me back to reality. Numb, tearless and speechless I stared at the place where moments ago a living burial had taken place.

It was all over!

Calmly and slowly I left the window where I had

watched and waited the last few hours of this dreary April morning.

What next?

I made my way to the staff bathroom. Here, no one would seek to follow me. I could be still, to think, to plan and to visualize the future. Here I could be alone with my God.

A sudden weakness came over me. The coldness within me began to melt slowly; I could no longer control myself—the breaking point had been reached. Fumbling for Father's large handkerchief in my uniform apron, I began to sob. At last I could let go—I had no power to control it and did not care. Hot, exhausted, but also wonderfully relieved, I contemplated the present situation. The safety and solitude of this bathroom became the springboard from which I would enter an entirely new world. Situations and experiences hitherto unknown would unfold themselves hour by hour. Determined to be courageous, alert and useful in the complex battle of self-preservation, I left the bathroom and entered a crazy world.

Chapter 7

Slowly, I made my way down the landing. As with Abraham, it was true also with me that day I went, not knowing where I was going (Hebrews 11:8). The babies played happily on the floor, and the toddlers enjoyed fun at their tables or in the indoor sandpit.

A young nurse approached me with the news that Matron wished to see me in the office. Indifferent to any decision likely to be made, I knocked at the office door. Without the slightest reference to the events of the past hours, Matron told me I was to go off duty that afternoon and use the time available to report to the Board of Guardians at the central headquarters in town. Being under age, the community was responsible for my movements and maintenance. A sudden thought flashed across my mind—the children, *our* children, they too had been fostered due to the arrest of their parents. Before tonight I, too, would be fostered out—I now was one of them.

Thanking Matron for her help, I started to leave. "Nurse Dobschiner," she called after me, "if you wish to continue your employment with us, we will be happy to have you. Please let me know once you are settled and do keep in touch."

Thanking her once more, I left the office and collected my coat and black leather case. I walked the streets for hours, and the long walk relieved the inner tension and helped me to come to terms and accept what had to be!

The streets were crowded, the vendors noisily shouted their wares, cars and trams rattled their way through the old narrow streets. I fought my way past them all, until an empty stomach reminded me that I had to eat. I knew one or two Jewish butchers in the center of our ghetto, and one who also served tea and rolls. The thought of Russian tea and rolls with sausage made my mouth water indeed, and automatically I walked faster. The shop was warm and people stood around the corner or sat on stools facing the narrow marble ledge along the wall.

I ordered tea and rolls and relaxed at a small table in the corner. I cupped both hands around the scalding hot stimulant, obtaining at the same time as much heat as possible from the glass itself. Dreamily I gorged myself —I was shivery, sleepy and not quite myself.

How long I used the hospitality of that butcher's shop I really do not know, but looks from the other customers made me feel I had outstayed my welcome. Gripping my black case firmly, I prepared to leave, since to stay any longer would only postpone the events which inevitably were awaiting me somewhere. At the counter I asked for more rolls with salami and liver sausage; these would be my standby for the rest of the day.

The Board of Guardians was a good bit away yet, and it took me until evening to reach the familiar building. People seemed to be everywhere; I was surrounded by worried faces, eyes red from sleeplessness and frequent crying. Children of all ages mingled with the grown-ups, their faces reflecting their stories of fear and bewilderment.

An official approached me. "Can I help you?" he asked in a most matter-of-fact tone. Not knowing if he really could, I told him all that had happened in the past twenty-four hours. Without the slightest sign of surprise, he was ready with the mechanical instructions: "Along the corridor, Room Three, please!"

Rather startled at his detached attitude, I made my way along the "sausage machine" to which I was now destined. At Room Three, another official asked the obvious questions and then handed me a card with details of my new foster parents. He smiled and wished me good luck.

Having a fairly long walk ahead of me to the southern part of the city, I set out at a steady pace in order to be there before curfew at eight o'clock. At last I reached my destination. The whole building had a modern appearance and looked bright and inviting. All the houses on both sides of the boulevard were built in the same style, with balconies on alternate stories.

Rather pleased, I climbed the broad, stone outside stairway, then rang the bell beside the nameplate "Rennie." An electric buzzer sounded and the door opened automatically. I entered, closed the door securely and climbed the carpeted stairway to the Rennie's flat. A kindly lady in her mid-forties invited me to enter. The private house door shut behind me.

Mrs. Rennie made coffee for us both while I told her all she wanted to know. At last she showed me my room. Incredible! I'd never had a room like this. It even had a balcony. If only my parents could have seen me here, their minds would have been at ease. Mrs. Rennie left me to settle in. The other members of the family would not be home till later and I would meet her husband and two grown-up daughters at dinner time.

Carefully I folded the luxurious eiderdown and laid it across the chair by the window. I stretched out on the bed and fell asleep before I could think or worry anymore. When I eventually wakened, the room light was on and the curtains drawn to hide the gloomy blackout material. A young girl, known to me later as Mirjam, stood beside the bed with a hot cup of tea. Yes, I was ready for it. We chatted about absolutely nothing and were almost relieved when Mrs. Rennie called us for dinner. A quick wash in the beautiful bathroom and I was ready for more introductions.

Without any fuss I was accepted into this home as one of the family. I was allowed all the freedom I could possibly enjoy under the circumstances. The conversation on this and other nights centered on the new arrests of the day, what news had been received from Westerborg, the central collecting camp, speculations about the immediate future and discussion about rumors and gossip in general.

Each morning I left after breakfast to start the long walk to my work in the nursery. Each day I gazed at the large glass swing doors of The Theater from which I had seen my parents depart for the last time. Each day the roll call of the little ones became smaller, as more and more were collected during the night. Each night, also, the volume of traffic increased. Each new day had its revelations of human misery and innocent suffering.

When off duty for an hour to two, I would walk along the Plantage Middelaan over the swing bridge and along the canal toward my old home. The occupants of the barge outside our house greeted me always with a serious, but understanding nod of the head. Often I felt tempted to speak to these, our former friendly neighbors, but, not wishing to endanger their safety, I held my peace. The house always looked forsaken, but one day, at the end of April, my heart thumped with shock and anger as I glanced toward our windows. No curtains were at the windows and the glass panes gaped a horrible bleakness at my staring, questioning gaze.

The gangway of the old barge squeaked. The son, Mr. Boran, came toward me and placed a hand on my shoulder, nodding his head repeatedly. "It happened this morning. They came with two vans. It took them all morning." I wasn't surprised. I did not want to cry anymore. Forcing a thank-you smile, I bade him good-bye.

As I walked away I visualized all that was gone. I thought about my old doll. She had been given to me when I left Berlin. She was then thirty-five years old—I'd grown to love her. What about our unique cuckoo clock? Would I ever see one like it again? The solid oak sideboard; the large box of Easter crockery and cutlery; my mother's personal treasures; the family albums—everything was irreplaceable.

When I described these happenings to the Rennies that evening their sympathy was with me during the first course of dinner, but soon the conversation resumed its normal trend—the arrests, the possibility of escape, the news from camps. My sorrow had not really touched them, my loss wasn't theirs, my interests unimportant where life was concerned. Perhaps they were right—all would be dust in the end.

CHAPTER 8

During the next few weeks, life settled down to a normal pattern. The days became almost monotonous. I left the house each morning early and worked quiet unrestricted hours at the nursery, leaving well after six in the evening. The long walk enabled me to reach home just before curfew. At dinner, the talk seemed so superficial—always the same subjects—I made it a point to retire early, where I could be alone with my thoughts and my memories.

One morning, I walked smartly toward the nursery as usual, when passers-by close to the building stopped me, recognizing my uniform. I was advised, strongly, not to proceed in that direction, but to change course and return it to the place I had come from. They did not give me much information, but what I did hear was sufficient to make me thank them gratefully. They had emptied the nursery during the night and commanded the staff to bring all the children into the lorries. Who could argue? Who could or would plead?

I returned to the Rennies. Mrs. Rennie was surprised to see me but took the news calmly. I crept to my room, my refuge, my heavenly solitude. Through the curtained windows I observed the hustle and bustle down below of the free people—the people in trams and private cars, the daily shoppers, the little children holding their mothers' hands or those still in prams. Where were *our* toddlers and babies?

The days were much longer now, the nights too. I couldn't sleep, having no long walks and hard work to engage in. Oh, yes, to help at home was a privilege I was now able to discharge fully; it paid some of the debt I owed this family. The payment from the Board of Guardians would never make up for the freedom I had enjoyed in their home.

There was no need to wait long. Monotony did not belong to our day and age. Sunday, the twentieth of June, became yet another terrible day for our people. Around nine o'clock in the morning one could hear noises—familiar, but uncommon in this area. It surely couldn't be true, not here in Amsterdam South? I did not dare to rise from my bed—I just listened to the sounds I had come to know so well—the roaring of army lorries, the screeching brakes of many trams, the harsh and almost hoarse voices of army officials and the tramp of their nail-studded boots. I just *had* to peep, just to get a glimpse of what was happening out there.

At each corner and other strategic points along the boulevard one could see the familiar green lorries, but there were also rows and rows of trams, all now standing motionless, ready for their cargo of human misery. From dozens of houses groups of men, women and children were emerging. It was strange to see it happening in daylight, to have sorrow and misery exposed to all the neighbors. All their faces looked shocked as they were driven towards lorry or tram. Many cried hysterically, others wiped their tears silently, but the children were so frightened. Parents tried to comfort them, but these little ones had to accept their lot in the same way as their parents. For them, too, there was no way out. I saw some youths trying to escape, but the soldiers were everywhere; they saw to it that no one escaped so that the final annihilation might be postponed.

In some strange way I realized that this day would be my day of arrest. Having no luggage, it was easy to be ready for whatever lay ahead. My small black case was always near; it only needed the addition of a few toilet articles.

While collecting these in the bathroom and studying my face in the mirror, the doorbell rang. I ran to the living room. My heart was pounding. All the Rennies were assembled there along with two Gestapo and a Dutch black-shirt who assisted the Germans with language problems or rather obstreperous victims.

The shout of *Alles mit* assured me of their errand. Mr. Rennie talked in German, showed them many documents, and unsuccessfully tried to humor them. Somehow his papers must have had a valid stamp which at last pacified the hunters; a stamp which would prolong the struggle for life a little longer.

They pointed to me: "And what about her? Who is she? What is she doing here?" They paused, waiting for Mr. Rennie's reply.

He could do nothing. "She only lives here. Her parents have already been arrested. . . ."

"Sic . . . mit." I knew it. It was all over now.

With a strange sigh of relief I said good-bye to the Rennies, thanking them for their kind hospitality. It seemed that for the first time in years, I walked in complete freedom. The strain and stress which went together with the fight for survival were no longer needed.

Quiet, relaxed, and at ease, I began to talk to my escorts as they led me down the two flights of stairs.

"Could I do anything to help you? I love children; would you like me to look after them?"

They still did not answer, but looked in amazement at one another and at me. So I tried again.

"Would you please speak to your Oberste and obtain permission to let me look after the children until we get to the station, where they can join their parents once more. There is a lot of confusion and unnecessary hardship for both parents and children during the journey."

No reply was given. By this time we were downstairs and I joined the stream of misery which made its way along the boulevard to the trams and lorries. Soldiers were everywhere: a voice from a loudspeaker was shouting orders at random. Then, in glad surprise, I heard: "Any parents who want their children to reach the station in comfort may hand them over to the nurse who is waiting in front of tram wagon 24. You will be reunited again before entering the station."

That nurse was I. They had listened after all! Little ones came, and, as they came, I loved each one and lifted each into my tram. Most of the children were over six years of age and all wore the large yellow star, and all had big labels tied to coats or jackets with full identity details.

Moving around in the tram, I talked to the little ones and smiled many a tear away. But oh, how bewildered was the atmosphere. One particular boy about eight years of age attracted me strangely. He just stood on the platform and stared unseeingly before him, not a tear on his face, unaware of anyone around him.

After my second round of the children, I ventured near him, and stood quietly beside him for a minute or two. Even my arm around his shoulder did not have any effect. As some children became restless I left him, only to return to that lonely little statue as quickly as I could. I glanced at his name tag, I took his little hand and said, "Harry, we'll stay close together, shall we?" Contact was established without a word from him, but his eyes softened—they were wet.

I began to sing, and some of the little ones smiled and joined in. We sang nursery rhymes, popular songs and school songs. The steady stream of people passing our tram had not stopped. Some looked up in sheer amazement as they heard our singing: others couldn't help smiling for a moment and we smiled back, yet every now and then a little one broke down and wept again.

The lorries, revving up their engines, began their deportation.

"All set?" A soldier asked.

"Yes, all set!" I replied. He jumped on the platform and gave a sign to the driver. Shaking and shuddering, the tram began to move slowly.

My children were silent now. They listened to the voices from outside. By now we had left the more familiar streets and were heading toward the station. We could see the platform from our tram. It was already jammed with people and baggage. The raid must have started very early indeed—or had they been sent from The Theater?

We stopped and filed out slowly, assisted by our soldier escorts. As the children left me to rejoin their parents, Harry remained by my side. Evidently, his parents must have been arrested some days before.

Soon we became part of a massive, seemingly endless, stream of people, all wearing the same glaring bright yellow star—men, women, children, babies—all pushing their way through the vestibule doors. As it became our turn to mount the tightly packed stairway, I noticed a tiny, beet-red face, packed into a pram amidst sacks and bundles of all descriptions. The mother pushed, while the father walked alongside, holding the hand of another child and carrying a toddler.

Urging Harry to stay near me, I made my way to the front of the pram, gripped the bodywork and inched up the stairs backward, trying to help the mother get her burden to the top.

We gained the platform, breathless but triumphant, and were swallowed up in the hopeless sea of humanity that milled about. The green uniforms of our oppressors were everywhere. After only a short wait, a great stir moved the crowd. Their voices swelled to a continual hum. This soon was drowned by the rattle of many wagons wheels on the rails beside our platform. It was a long freight train; I could not even see the last car. The full length of the platform was now filled by the gaping bleakness of each car, sliding doors wide open to receive their loads. The iron bars hung from their joints, soon to be used to secure us inside.

Unconsciously, we endeavored to stay in the open a

little longer. We fussed about the pram; we attended to the now bitterly crying baby; we fastened the shoes of the little ones, as the voices of the soldiers thundered through the crowd *"Einsteigen, schnell-einsteigen."* Without the slightest resistance the crowds moved forward into their gaping wagons—almost fifty in one wagon is a good guess. Then the heavy sliding doors rolled shut and the iron bars were clicked into position. Fresh air to meet the needs of these people filtered through the five-inch gap at the center of each door. Although many hundreds had left the platform, it still seemed to be as crowded as ever.

At last it was our turn! Harry jumped in ahead of us. We lifted the little ones in and he held their hands. The father followed, then the mother, and we lifted the pram into the cattle truck. It was packed inside. The sliding doors rammed shut, plunging us all into momentary darkness, then, slowly, the five inches of daylight penetrated through the gloom. I thought of the iron bar in position on the outside.

I loosened the baby's bonnet. She was soaking with perspiration and pimply-red where her bonnet had been. Heat spots? Flea bites? A sudden strange impulse flooded my whole being. Spots! Cupping my hands I shouted at the top of my voice through the few inches available to me, "Attention, attention. Infectious disease. Open the doors at once. Danger! Highly infectious family in this wagon. Hurry! Hurry!

The voices of the crowd outside swelled, and moments later fresh air and light were with us once more. As the officials faced me I ordered them to "stand aside please, gangway, please, scarlet fever!" Walking to the baffled parents, I lifted the pram and stepped backward onto the platform. The family followed and Harry too.

"Over to the waiting room!" a high official pointed to a glass sectional cubicle at the far end of the platform. "Nurse, you are in charge and responsible for that family."

Suddenly we were alone, for the first time that day. We looked at one another and smiled wryly. We could not speak for a long time. I placed the bonnet back on the baby's head in order to retain the spots.

Soon a doctor arrived—one of us.

Showing him my patient I said questioningly, seeking for confirmation, "Scarlet fever?" He asked if I was alone, and if I was willing to work with him. My desire had at last been granted. I was a nurse in action.

"Have you any instruments?" he asked. Proudly I opened my little black case where my treasures were hidden—my own private medical case and first-aid box. He smiled. "Right, Nurse, busy yourself. Take the baby's temperature. I'll be back shortly."

For the first time I lifted the little girl from her mountain of clothes, luggage and packages. She felt hot and damp. I cuddled her against me, talking and laughing; she soon smiled as well. So did her father and mother, but not my poor wee Harry.

As I took the baby's temperature, the doctor returned and showed his approval with a smile. "How is she?" he asked.

Without checking the mercury I replied, "101.2, poor little lamb." He looked on for a moment as I dressed her and handed her back to the parents.

He then called me to the other part of the waiting room. "Bring into this place anyone you can find, anyone who, in your opinion, is 'ill.' Be careful and judge aright. See what you can do, Nurse. I'll look along every now and then. Perhaps we can get some folks out of this, but be careful."

We went in different directions, looking to see where we were needed. Incredible and unforgettable was our patroling along that platform. One felt so helpless to answer the many cries, "Nurse, my mother, please look at her. Oh, what can we do?"

Making my way along the stairway I saw another family huddled together for comfort. "Hullo," I addressed a little one, who immediately turned away from yet another uniform. Her parents were obviously exhausted as well. What could possibly count for an excuse to keep this family out of the train? No apparent reason. Patting the head of the little girl, and pushing the damp hair off her hot forehead, I noticed pimples once more, watery eyes and a running red nose. Could this be the real thing? Either chicken pox or measles? Hurrah, this seemed a worthwhile catch.

"Come along this way; you will be more comfortable where I take you." They followed me without a word, and we fought our way through the dense crowd until we reached the waiting room.

Dr. van Ebo was there attending to other true casualties.

As we walked in, I announced "another infection." "Over there, Nurse." He pointed to the still unoccupied part of the waiting room. As soon as he was free he came over to inspect my latest patient.

"Yes, Nurse, that's measles all right. Well done."

Delighted with the compliment, I attempted to go fishing once more, but a sudden stir made me stop. Cries of despair and fear arose from the crowd, as if in reply to the cries from within the cattle trucks as the long trail of wagons left the station.

While the crying was still at its height and the last wagon still within sight, I left the waiting room with a derisive purpose: to rescue at all costs whoever seemed a deserving case. Humanly, who could decide? We had to be quick and move fast: this would be our last chance. The next lot of wagons would surely clear the platform.

I searched among the crowds. There was a woman heavy with child. "What are you doing here?" I shouted. "You are almost due. You should have proper care! Come this way, please."

She replied calmly and with a smile, "Oh no, I'm only seven months."

"No, you're nine," I objected.

"What about my brother?" Pathetically she pointed to the man at her side.

"Your husband," I emphasized. "He must come with you at a time like this. Come quickly."

Once more we wound our way through the dense crowds, still climbing those broad stairways. It seemed as if no one had left; the platform filled up continually.

Dr. van Ebo was busy when I arrived. I explained about my latest catch, and we went into fresh consultation.

He explained his plans simply, step by step. We hoped and prayed in our hearts that all would go well and safety would be the portion of those we had rescued, and for ourselves.

"I've asked for an ambulance to transfer the people to our hospital. We must go with them, then return and collect the rest. They won't allow us more than one ambulance. Until it arrives we must make ourselves useful, but we can't rescue any more or suspicion will be aroused.

"Try to leave the station. Be resolute, be quick, be determined. Look busy at all times. Keep your aim in mind, as you will have to deal with many roadblocks and soldiers. Your job is to mislead.

"Make for the hospital, get strong disinfectant, and return to the station. Explain that you want this place clean and safe for normal service tomorrow. That is to be your explanation during your journey. Will you try?

"Now, good luck. We'll meet again, I hope!"

As he turned to his work and I to mine, I wondered why he chose me to pass into freedom. Did he want me to stay out, or did he want a peg on which to hang genuine excuses to questioning officials?

Running downstairs, two at a time, I was confronted by my first roadblock. "Halt!" he shouted.

Speaking in German I told him, "Don't you realize that up on that platform we have various infectious diseases and not a drop of disinfectant? A shocking situation." I shocked him further by requesting transport for myself to the hospital and back. He was furious and told me to get out of his way, which I gladly did.

Twice more I had to face such obstacles before I reached the street. I marched along, explaining my errand to each soldier who stopped me—miraculously, all let me by! When I reached the hospital at last, no one could be bothered to listen. Finally I located a bottle of disinfectant and left as unnoticed as I had come.

After some hours I reached home sweet home, but

how dreadfully empty was our platform. Trains had come and gone, clearing the station of all the human misery of the early afternoon. My heart beat faster, and anxiety overcame me. What about Dr. van Ebo? How silly I looked on that empty platform with that large bottle of Lysol.

Almost mechanically, I walked the length of the platform toward our waiting room. How empty it now was! Thank God I saw figures, yet, not all. Tired and worn out, Dr. van Ebo explained how matters stood.

"One ambulance has left. We must wait for its return, then busy ourselves in helping these people onto stretchers and chairs, down in the lift and into the ambulance. We must stay with them, Nurse, very close, or we'll have had it after all. Understand what I mean?"

Thank goodness we did not have to wait too long for the ambulance. The men came toward us from the station lift carrying their stretchers. They viewed the situation in the waiting room and had some quiet words with each other. Yes, they would disregard regulations and red tape. We all would have to go in that ambulance. It was too dangerous to leave anyone behind for they would surely be transferred to The Theater to await the next deportation to the camps.

Leaving the large bottle of Lysol as a monument, we all descended in that lift, making our way to the ambulance watched by half a dozen soldiers who didn't speak one word.

Gratefully, we looked at one another when the doors were shut and the ambulance moved off on the beginning of our journey away from yet another nightmare.

CHAPTER 9

In the reception hall of the hospital, formalities took over once more. The sick and not so sick were split up into respective units for care and treatment. Soon Dr. van Ebo and I were alone once more.

"Have you somewhere to go, Nurse?" he asked with concern.

"Not really, Doctor. Don't worry, I'll be all right. I'll go to my friend's room and spend the night there. No one will object, I am sure."

"Well," he replied, "you go to your friend's room and tell her about our expectant mother." (We had previously discovered that she was Sister Henny's sister-in-law! Quite incredible, among all those thousands!)

No one replied to my knock at Sister Henny's door. Hesitantly, I ventured in. A mighty weariness came over me. Noticing some blankets, I wrapped them round me, stretched out on the floor, and slept soundly. Next morning I wakened as Sister Henny knelt beside me with a fresh roll and hot mug of tea.

"You've got to tidy yourself and put on one of my aprons, Hansie. Matron wants you in her office by half-past ten!" she said.

Having washed my face, tidied my clothes, combed my hair, and put on one of my friend's aprons, I looked fairly respectable. She nodded, with a smile of approval.

"Well then, Hansie, let's go. I'll show you Matron's office." Sister Henny led the way. It only seemed a moment or two before I faced the door. "Good luck!" she said, then I was alone.

I knocked politely and a voice said, "Come in." There then was the Queen of Hearts. She didn't look like a matron to me: just like an ordinary woman with a uniform on. But, oh, once she opened her mouth, she was no ordinary woman. After I had wished her good morning she answered with a reprimand in a none too quiet voice. "Since when have my nurses begun to wear earrings?"

Quietly I enlightened her that I was not "one of her nurses" but belonged to the Creche across from The Theater.

Her voice softened as she replied, and I could detect a faint smile.

"Dr. van Ebo has spoken to me about you and has told me what you did yesterday. From today onwards you are one of my nurses!"

How could one hug such a woman? I was almost beside myself with happiness. A real nurse in a real hospital! I must have beamed all over, for all of a sudden Matron gave a big broad smile. "Please go now with my assistant who will show you your quarters and then direct you to your ward. Sister Henny will answer any of your queries after duty tonight. Good-day, Nurse."

"Thank you, thank you very much, Matron. I will do my very best," was all I had time to say.

The assistant matron left me at the end of a long, dark corridor with many doors. "Please report to 'infectious diseases' after lunch. You'll find your way to the dining room and to the ward. Just keep asking." She was gone. Here was *my* room! I had to let off steam. I jumped, danced and bounced on the bed, throwing pillows ceilingward and cuddling them against me a moment later.

Now, off to the dining room. I would follow my nose: the aroma indicated that it couldn't be far away! I heard the clatter of dishes and soon I was following other nurses who all seemed to be going purposefully in the same direction. Having reached the dining room I watched the others and did exactly what they did, taking part in the general routine as if I'd lived there for years. A full dinner free of charge! I ate every bite and was thankful.

On the way out I asked directions to "infectious diseases." The smell of Lysol was prominent, and the nurses behind the glass-walled cubicles wore masks. I came to a halt before a Sister who told me I would have to wear a special coverall each time I entered the ward. She explained my duties and said that that afternoon I would mainly observe my fellow nurses and lend a hand wherever it was needed. That night, I thought over the events of these last few days. So much had happened since Sunday morning, yet tonight I felt so clean, so happy, so grateful. I was a nurse!

Next morning I was in the ward early, ready for anything. I was told to help with bedmaking, tidying, dusting, serving midmorning drinks, giving medicines, and then I was shown how to give injections. On my first morning! And many more important duties had to be attended to by responsible juniors, for trained staff was now so scarce.

The most noticeable thing about the patients was that they all had something in common—a broken heart. Even the nursing staff, affected by this same symptom, showed a greater understanding and compassion to those around them than in normal times. Having a common bond, sharing a common loss, gave us a common desire to help one another with comfort and courage, and during these next few weeks I learned a great deal.

On the fifth day of July another rumor of arrests sounded among the staff. These rumors were confirmed by a voice over the loudspeaker system. "Attention, attention. Any members of the staff of this hospital who has been engaged in work of any kind under this roof for three months or less, are asked to assemble in the gardens for an important announcement. Please come immediately and without delay in order to avoid the disruption of daily routine."

I left the ward, but walked along dozens of corridors to give myself time to think. Would this battle never end? There was that loudspeaker again: "Will the junior staff assemble in the gardens for a special announcement. Please make your way to the gardens."

Orderlies in white coats hurried alongside nurses—obviously married couples and lovers who had sought shelter and work in the hospital. Their faces bore the familiar expression of fear.

The gardens were crowded. Couples and friends stood hand in hand, awaiting the inevitable. We all looked at the group of men from the Board who stood beside several high-ranking Gestapo. Each of them held books, papers or lists in his hands.

"Ladies and gentlemen, due to overstaffing here in this hospital and shortage of staff in the work camps, we are duty bound to alter this unequal situation. We have, therefore, decided to move the newer members of the staff. This seems only fair. We shall, therefore, read out in alphabetical order the names of those we require today. If your name is called please go to your room at once and return with your rucksack to the front of the building, where transport is awaiting you. We ask for your cooperation to carry out this transfer in a quick and efficient manner." Very cleverly explained, and how politely put! Everyone knew what was really behind all that talk; compulsory arrest!

I didn't need to wait very long. The letter D was soon reached and Hans Dobschiner's name was called. Following the other "chosen laborers" I made for my room. The rucksack, which most of my people owned, I had lost long ago, but my little black case would go with me as it had done before. I saw no one I knew. Where could Sister Henny be? Was everyone keeping out of the way to make the parting easier? I didn't know and I didn't care anymore. I walked down the stone flight of stairs without looking to the right or left. I walked out through the heavy wooden doors which were now open wide, as if for ambulance traffic. Two steps on the pavement and I was ushered into a lorry.

Around me were only elderly people, many with bandages or plasters. These rogues! They had not only rounded up staff in the back gardens, but elderly patients had been arrested too, probably from day rooms or convalescing wards.

I sat down on the bench and looked around in order to fix my eyes on someone for just a little smile. Yes, it was possible. Several smiled back at "nurse." Did they perhaps feel a sense of security because a nurse was in their midst? Although we all were birds within a cage, wings securely clipped, yet one could always hope for deliverance.

The tailgate of the lorry clicked into position, pegs into bolts, and off we went. What would our destination be today? Where would we be unloaded? I felt quite hungry and wondered about my fellow travelers. Some licked their lips, others sweets—a most treasured possession indeed. "Give us this day our daily bread" was an unspoken thought.

The lorry did not travel too fast. One could look at streets, houses, people, and photograph the dear familiar city scenes on one's memory. After leaving the familiar streets and the shopping center, the journey became bumpy and the lorry jolted along faster over uneven cobbled roads. To my great surprise, we made for the dock area, and its railway line.

As soon as we left the lorries we were directed to our part of the train. This time it consisted of carriages for human cargo, eight to one compartment. Only the elderly were with me. Not knowing just what to do, I smiled again. It wasn't long before we were conversing freely, feeling as if we belonged to one another. It was a pleasant sensation.

Now and again someone would go to the window and keep us informed of what was happening. A happy atmosphere developed; it could have been an outing of the Senior Citizens' Club! An elderly gentleman informed us that a soup trolley was on its way. The thought of hot soup made everyone's mouth water. How wonderful! It was not long till we received our share and we soon emptied the mugs to the last drop before wrapping them once more securely among our luggage. When would they be used again?

An elderly lady inquired in rather a loud voice in which ward I had been on duty. When I told her she jumped in horror, pleading with me to leave them rather than "pass anything on."

"Please, Nurse, be understanding. It's not that we have anything against you personally; it is just that we could not face an infectious illness; we are so weak already. Please, Nurse, leave our compartment. Please leave us."

A sure contradiction of all circumstances! I wasn't allowed out of that train, yet they wanted me to leave. We all had an idea of our immediate future, yet they worried about a nurse from the isolation unit being in their midst. It did not make sense!

They kept on pleading: "Please go; please leave us." Was this the Almighty's constraining command? Ought I to go? Out there, to face assault or even death for leaving the train? "All right, I'll go," I told them.

Bidding them good luck and taking my case, I opened the door and stepped onto the platform like a free woman. At once a soldier approached me, but I stepped toward him in a firm and determined manner as if he had been my aim from the very beginning. Ignoring the pointing rifle, I opened the conversation, smiling helplessly. "It's no use; they won't have me anywhere in the train. They are frightened, you see, because I worked in the isolation unit with the infectious diseases. What on earth can we do? I think I'd better go back to the hospital. The trouble is it's so far away. Have you any transport going in that direction? I'd be most grateful for your help."

Rattling all this off in one breath in a flat Berlin accent must have taken him completely by surprise. He lowered his gun and turned to a passing soldier. "Are you going back to the city? Drop this nurse at the hospital, will you? Thanks."

Turning to me his only command was: "Follow that soldier, Nurse." Trying not to show too much delight or surprise I stepped in a matter-of-fact way toward his friend, bidding my liberator a comradely good-bye.

This time my journey was most remarkable, traveling solo with a soldier in an army truck to—freedom.

My driver dropped me at the front entrance. I shudder to think what fear and consternation the sight of that lorry must have created in the imaginations of those who noticed our arrival and heard the screech of the brakes. What rumors must have passed from mouth to mouth for the second time that day. Yet, only I stepped out!

Thanking my driver escort, I walked toward the door which at last was shut. All morning it had been wide open while people were carried out or speeded on their way to the unknown.

This time I, only I, returned, and no one seemed surprised to see me or made any move to welcome me back. One was almost shy to be free or still alive, for it was always one more person to account for or get rid of. The enemy demanded a certain number of people; they had to be supplied. If they insisted that the staff should be larger than a specified number, then this too had to be obeyed explicitly. Therefore, today I was the odd one out, an embarrassment to my hospital.

"Sorry, but I'd love to live a little longer," I thought; "just a little while."

It seemed only proper to report to Matron first. Calmly she addressed me with the words, "Well, Nurse, so you are back. Go to the kitchen and get something to eat and then go back to your ward."

"Thank you, Matron." No questions were asked; no feelings shown. I became part of the machinery once more.

Amid the hustle and bustle of the main kitchen's activity I enjoyed a good and peaceful meal. It was as invigorating as that last meal of rolls with salami which

I had enjoyed in the little butcher's shop before I reported to the Board of Guardians.

My room had not been reoccupied, so I took possession of it as though nothing had happened. A little wash, a clean apron, and I reported for duty as if nothing special had happened that day.

The next few weeks were uneventful. No major raids, only sad little incidents but of great importance for those involved. Unconsciously, one settled into the safe routine of hospital life, almost deleting from one's mind the thought of any possible upheaval.

One would not dream of leaving the grounds when off duty. One would not dream either of ever wearing anything else but a uniform. The hospital and its uniform were still the only visible protection from the enemy.

Our city streets were the hunting ground for any soldier who wanted a game—the game of terrifying anyone who wore the compulsory bright yellow star of David.

I felt stricken and almost at my wit's end when Matron called me to her office one morning and put me on district duty. She emphasized the great need for more staff for this type of work. The hospital had a great percentage of sham sickness, made up of people who had gone there to escape arrest at home or at work. Consequently, the really sick could not get the beds or care they needed—hence the team of district nurses required for this job.

Matron did explain it so well. It sounded perfectly logical, but I had felt so happy and secure inside. . . .

It was not long, however, before the vision of the ill folks at home gripped my imagination. They were really ill and needed nursing care twenty-four hours a day. They were in pain and in fear, and lonely too. Yes, I would go. Of course I would go. Matron explained the condition of the female patient she had designated to my care. "A young woman, acute pneumonia, needing careful attention and injections." She was to be my responsibility. I, in turn, would be responsible to her home physician.

Fear and disappointment left me altogether once I knew myself entrusted with that young life. I went back to my room, packed a few belongings, and reported to the district superintendent for detailed instructions. I was proud of my outdoor uniform, and the waist-length black veil to which I now had been promoted. The bright yellow star shone brighter still from the background of my dark blue garb; but I learned to walk tall! Twice a day I had to brave the danger of the streets to go on duty and return nightly to my hospital room. Twice a day!

Eagerly I made for the address given to me. Mr. Sim showed me the house and my room and, before he left for work we had a luncheon snack together over which we got better acquainted. It was easy to roll up my sleeves and get the house in order; to do many a chore which, up till now, had to be left undone. It wasn't long before my patient and I became quite close and true friends.

Soon this new routine became part of my life. I enjoyed it. Their home was looked upon as my home, and they did all in their power to make me happy.

No one mentioned days off. One was not concerned with regular hours. One was on duty, and glad to be kept occupied.

Summer, 1943: raids and rumors of raids, day and night. Always bad news reached our ears; never a letup. The enemy steadily continued its program of annihilation. Our numbers decreased hour by hour. Whenever Mr. Sim returned from work, he told us of raids and arrests.

We had been together for nearly one month when Mr. Sim returned from work long before the usual time. This meant trouble. Ashen-faced and breathless, he burst into the flat. "They are doing the N.I.Z., your hospital. It's dreadful. All those sick folk and the whole staff. It is said they won't leave anyone behind today. Nurse, don't leave this house in uniform. Don't leave at all. You must stay with us. They would arrest you at once. The population is filled with rage. Rumors of a general strike are on everybody's lips."

I had heard enough. Excusing myself, I went to the bathroom, the only place I could have true privacy and silent meditation. I could see, in my mind's eye, all those familiar faces; the terror that must undoubtedly be theirs at this very moment; the elderly, baffled and bewildered; the children, crying and calling for their mothers; others fighting and kicking to be left alone. I'd seen it so often. Methodically, coldbloodedly, the wards would be emptied. The staff would be compelled to help in this hellish scheme. Then they, too, would find themselves in the army lorries.

Another chapter had just ended in my struggle for survival. Was it worthwhile? The possibilities of escaping ultimate arrest seemed so remote. The chances narrowed continually. Finally my turn would surely come.

However, there was nothing to be done at present. No plans could be made, no ventures undertaken. One had to remain hidden until the raids had died down, or I would be an escape suspect. As long as they didn't approach the houses at the same time we were safe. We were like mice caught in a trap.

When I returned to the dining room the coffee was made, the atmosphere quiet and relaxed. This time they seemed entirely concerned for *me*. "Nurse, you can stay with us as long as you want. Look on this place as your home. Come in and out as you like." And he added with a smile, "When it is safe to do so."

A week seemed long enough for self-imposed house arrest. Soon I began to venture out, cautiously at first, but aiming always a little farther from home. One learned to listen for rumors, to search for scraps of genuine news. One looked for authoritative guidance among the chaos of social community life. Amazingly, a clue of leadership was found, and I searched for definite information.

Unofficially, the Board searched for survivors from the thirteenth of August raid in order to establish a skeleton staff for those who remained in the large, glass-fronted modern home for the aged in the center of Amsterdam. They wanted to turn this into an emergency hospital for the time being, having both services running side-by-side.

Could there be a vacancy for me? The only way to find out was to try, so I presented myself before one of the older Sisters of N.I.Z., who startled me by reproaching me for my delay in reporting for duty. She ordered me to report for duty as soon as my patient could dispense with my services, preferably by Friday night so that I could go on duty for the weekend. No free time—but the privilege of being free from arrest!

I reported for duty the end of August. The junior staff lived together in a huge dormitory, our bedside lockers our only privacy, but the atmosphere was harmonious and we all enjoyed the companionship. On my birthday, my roommates surprised me with as good a party as they could manage—they sang birthday songs and several managed to produce pancakes and sugar. It was a birthday to remember.

The days were uneventful, until one morning at the beginning of September when the night porter, just going off duty, called me over to the reception desk. "Dobschiner," he said, "would you like a chance of survival? I've got an address for you. Think about it quickly and see me tomorrow at this time."

He was gone, leaving me shaking like a leaf. Me, go underground? How could I? I had no funds, no financial backing, no connections. Why had he approached me? Just me? I had to keep this to myself. Absolute secrecy was a necessity.

Throughout the day I could not concentrate on the work I loved so much, my people, those who depended on me for care and attention. They and the staff seemed to notice that I was different, that something must have happened; yet I could not tell them.

By late afternoon my imagination had worked itself into a frenzy. I was frightened for the first time regarding the future. It seemed that a trap had been set, and there was no escape. Raids and arrests could be dodged, but when one was attacked along the "silent road" of so-called security, well, where then was there a way out?

Once off duty I sat in the dormitory, staring into the unknown future, endeavoring to get my position and the facts quite clear in my own mind. Weighing the pros and cons of a chance for survival I realized that, humanly speaking, I had none. I had no one to turn to, no possessions, no money, no connections: a nobody with only the will to live and work for those who needed help.

The will to live? Did I *have* the will to live? Was it worth it? Those I wanted to help, those too, would soon be gone. After all, this and this only was Hitler's final goal—the annihilation of all Jews. Why then fight to live? It would only be for a little while.

My willpower was weakening and once it began to slip the couldn't-care-less attitude was just around the corner. There was only one way open. If I surrendered voluntarily and reported to the labor camp authorities, they might give me a position as a nurse in the camp, and by working there I might gain survival. It was a risk, but also a chance I had to take. I couldn't continue on the basis of today's approach by the night porter. I was trapped both ways and could only free myself by deliberately reporting for voluntary arrest.

Yes, that was the answer. I would report at The Theater in the Plantage Middelaan. When? I was not too sure. Sometime that week. Probably quite suddenly, when I felt I could not go on any longer.

A fine young nurse sharing my dormitory sought my confidence. Repeatedly, she insisted that I tell her my troubles, but words could not be found for a long, long time. Yet she talked, and talked, and talked, repeatedly tempting me to speak. Soon I could resist no longer. Sobbing brokenly I told her of my continual escape during all these months, the fierce reality of the ultimate future for us all, and now the new proposal of the night porter. Why had he chosen me? I had no financial means. I was nothing to him or anyone. I was so frightened. I could not fight for survival much longer. I was tired; oh so tired. I wanted to surrender! I would go to The Theater tomorrow and then . . . I would travel the road all my family had taken. Yes, I would surrender.

Silence reigned for some time after my confession. Her longing to help was great, but what could she say? We both knew that I had spoken the truth.

Contemplatively, she endeavored to reason with me: "But Hansie, the way to The Theater is a deliberate act of suicide. You know it, and you must fight it. Accept the night porter's offer. There is just a chance that some way out is awaiting you. Some people don't need to pay for their keep, but just work for their living. Don't dwell too much on how a life of hiding will work out for you. Just take a day at a time."

But this cat-and-mouse game had lasted too long. I was finished. I couldn't fight anymore. There and then I decided that the next day, the sixth of September, would be the day on which I would commit my "deliberate act of suicide," as Lena had called it. Just before curfew, I would report at The Theater and, with a little bit of luck, would surprise my father and be with him on his birthday, the eighth.

While on duty on that last day of freedom, my mind was not on my work, not with my patients. I experienced a strange sensation. I was on duty, yet I was not there. I was away, far away from Amsterdam, among the milling thousands in trains and camps. I was part of despair, part of lost humanity, part of damnation and annihilation, part of equipment for the enemy's game.

Oh God, enter this hell and deliver me. I don't want to breathe anymore.

"I can't; I won't. Please receive me into Thy safety and peace. . . ."

Lena stood beside me, a syringe in her hand. "I said, for Mrs. Shand." How many times had she told me to give that injection? I hadn't heard her. She looked at me worriedly and replaced the syringe carefully in the kidney dish, resting the needle carefully on a pad of cotton wool.

I was crying inwardly, swallowing hard to avoid an outward display of grief. Lena, sensing that I couldn't keep up much longer, ordered me to leave the ward at once.

"Go to your dormitory, Hansie. Cry hard. Get it out of your system. It won't be long till dinner time, and I'll see you then."

I almost ran through the ward and along the corridors to the dormitory. My bed was a haven of rest and safety. I threw myself on its cool sheets, pushed my face into the pillow and cried as though these were the last tears I would shed before leaving this world. I sobbed long and fiercely, till, gradually, I felt the releasing of tension. Yes, I would do it—tonight. Calmly I considered my course of action. I would pretend that all was normal, not to arouse suspicion. I would act in a gay and carefree manner for the rest of the day, avoiding my fellow nurses, especially Lena.

"Wash your face, Hansie; get ready for dinner." The bell would go any moment. "Get moving. It's a long way to the dining hall!" The night porter came to my mind. He would be in bed now. There would be no questions asked as I passed the porter's office.

Blithely I skipped along the corridor, down the stairs, and through the front vestibule. No, it could not be—the night porter on day duty. What could I do? Would he notice me? A big broad smile on his face compelled me to go toward him. Don't worry, I encouraged myself. Tonight I would be free! Free? Well, I meant finished. It would all be over pretty soon.

"Good-day, Nurse! Well? Decided?" He waited pleasantly for my reply.

Sighing, I told him that it couldn't be done. I had no means of support, no places I knew, and no need for self-preservation as all my people were gone. "No, sir, no, please leave me alone." He let me go; almost sadly, I thought. Why should a complete stranger worry about me? I could not understand it.

Dinner was good, but I had always enjoyed what we got to eat. The food was warm and tasty. I said grace and gave thanks sincerely for those meals, meaning every word. What a blessing to have this daily food. During dinner my thoughts were far off once more.

Where would I eat tomorrow? Would I eat at all? Was I prepared to give up this daily luxury? I ate and ate as never before. Lena eyed me suspiciously. I was very excited but tried to hide it. Successfully?

The injections had to be given, the inhalations attended to, the compresses changed, poultices in position, beds made and tidied over and over again: the evening tea served, the invalids fed, bedpans given, oh dear, no break! The afternoon had been hectic. Would I ever get away? Now or never. Carefully, I placed the tray with glasses on the center table, then, without looking at either patient or nurse, I left the ward swiftly.

My heart was thumping as I ran up those stairs two at a time. In the dormitory I calmly collected my few private papers and possessions in my small black case. There was my nurse's coat, my veil, my gloves. Without any more thought I hurried down those familiar stairs, through the front vestibule, past the porter's office and outside.

Phew! I had managed it. I walked firmly and purposely toward my goal. The Theater! My mind was blank, with no thought of the possible consequences entering my head. I saw no one and nothing—I just walked on and on and on.

Twenty minutes must have passed as I turned the corner of the street which would bring me to the door of The Theater. Suddenly a hand on my shoulder brought me back to reality. Lena! She couldn't speak. She was red, perspiring profusely, panting like a dog after a hunt. While fighting to get her breath and searching for words, she began to cry.

Now it was my turn to be concerned for her. She gave me no chance, but pulled me back round the corner. She was furious.

"You selfish, stupid, childish idiot! Get back at once and stop your nonsense!" Looking at her watch she almost pulled me along the street. We had to hurry to be in on time.

I went back; ashamed, embarrassed, and as tame as a lamb.

On the stroke of eight we entered the J.I., breathless and exhausted.

"Go to your dormitory and get into bed," she ordered.

I obeyed.

CHAPTER 10

The early morning bell rang through the nurses' quarters. I had been awake for a while thinking over the happenings of the previous night; I realized I was fortunate to be there, to be lying in a cozy warm bed. Had it not been for Lena where would I be now? I would pull myself together and try to be brave once more. In the coming days I would work well and cause my friend no more distress. I was so ashamed.

Quietly I carried out my morning routine. Everyone behaved in a normal way, and I realized that Lena had not spoken to anyone about last night's incident. This increased my determination to work well.

At lunch I approached the hall porter myself. He smiled as usual.

"Well, Jan, I'd like to go, tomorrow, if you just tell me what to do. If this is to be the way for me I won't resist any longer."

Tomorrow was the deadline. He had to find a girl before the next day, as the cook's daughter, who should have gone, was still in bed with influenza. He had chosen me as the substitute to fill the gap.

"Nurse, you are dreaming. You must listen very carefully in case my duty is changed, and I do not see you again. You will leave immediately after lunch tomorrow, telling no one, not even your best friend, that you won't be back. You will leave the J.I. as if you were going for a walk. Take only the bare essentials and your handbag. This is important. You will go to this street and number, which you must memorize before leaving this building. You will walk smartly all the way—do not linger or talk to anyone. On approaching the street corner get ready to sneeze. That is, with your right hand take out a large handkerchief from your right-hand coat pocket, then, using both hands, thus moving your handbag upwards and over your star, sneeze at the precise moment of turning the corner. From then on keep your star covered till you have reached the memorized number and are safely inside the house. That's all!"

The eighth of September, 1943, was a dry day; at intervals the sun shone; there was a gentle breeze. A perfect day for the great event. Eagerly I attended to the morning chores. Purposefully, I dressed some patients, bed-bathing the invalids and elderly. We served their dinner, then settled them for their afternoon nap. Incredible how quickly the hours had passed!

Pretending to ignore the porter, I lifted my coat from a hook in the vestibule and stooped to take my black case from a cupboard in his office. As I stooped, I heard him repeating the address once more. "Good luck, Nurse," he wished me quickly. "Thank you, Jan," I said, then I walked through the swing door.

I felt somewhat diffident ringing the doorbell at the given address. What would I say? Whom would I face? As soon as the front door was shut behind me, I seemed to be under orders that needed no reply. "Come right upstairs. Please enter this room and sit down," the woman who admitted me said.

I sat for almost fifteen minutes in absolute silence. Then the front door slammed. Someone came upstairs, I was sure, but then silence again. I was startled at the suddenness with which the door behind me opened.

I rose to my feet, which was just as well for I was faced by the tallest man I had ever seen. He smiled almost sheepishly as he tried to make me feel at home. "Sit down, please," he urged. He appeared kindly, but came straight to the point as if time were most precious.

"What is your name?" he inquired. When I told him, he changed it to "Francisca." My new name was born!

"We'll make it Frans for short. Do you like that?" It was difficult to smile and say yes, but smile I did.

"Well, Frans, you will come with me. All right?" I was taken aback. Raising my eyebrows and frowning, I sought for words to express my doubts about such a life, my fears regarding money, and, generally, the unknown quantity of such a strange life.

He swept my doubts aside. I wondered who he was. Perhaps a secret agent of the enemy? Security did not seem to worry him. Would he take me to H.Q. straight from here? I'd heard of such happenings—medical guinea pigs or mistresses for the officers' mess! Oh my God, what had I done! Was I in the wrong hands after all?

Oh, yes, his eyes seemed honest enough, or what could be seen of them. They were tired and red-rimmed, as if sleep had not been his companion for some time. His forearms resting on his knees, his hands folded as in prayer, he looked right into my eyes and talked in a most persuasive manner.

"You must come, Frans. You owe it to your family, your parents, all your people. We want to save as many people as we can, to live a healthy normal life once the war is over. You can serve your people better if you stay in this country. We will look after you. Don't worry about money; that will come all right. There are so many interested in you and your people. They give donations voluntarily for your keep. You must come; they expect me to bring one girl today. It should have been the cook's daughter; all was fixed for her escape, but because of her illness you were chosen. We don't have much time, my dear. We get the three o'clock train from Central Station."

Words would not come, and still he talked on and on and on, pulling his chair nearer and nearer. I sat with head bent, staring into space, not noticing that little scissors were now in his hand.

He reached out to the coat I was wearing, cutting loose the star which labeled me a Jew, an outlaw, one of the condemned.

Was I paralyzed? Why did I not stop him? How could he dare do this? Without the star I could not show myself outside this house.

It was all over in seconds. He coughed, loudly and deliberately. The door of the room opened, and the lady who had shown me in, entered. Wonderingly I saw my star in her hand. Moments later I heard the flushing of her toilet. This was the end. I had no choice. Only one way lay open. I had to go with this stranger.

Mrs. X., whose name I have never learned, entered once more, carrying a red flannel dress. Smilingly, she wondered if it would fit me.

The tall stranger left us while I tried it on. Then "Daddy Long-Legs" was called in once more. He seemed pleased with the quick and effective transformation.

Then came a short list of instructions.

"You will walk with me as if on a sightseeing tour of Amsterdam. You speak German? All the better! Speak German only; it will make people turn from us in disgust. A perfect alibi! I will ask you about some buildings we pass. You will enlighten me as my guide, but in German only, please. We will go by tram to the station. Try to look as if you are used to it. Laugh and act normally. I am the stranger; you the German girl showing me around Amsterdam.

"Good-bye, my dear, and good luck." Did I detect tears in Mrs. X's eyes when we shook hands?

"Good-bye, and thank you very much." I had spoken at last.

The tall stranger now turned to me. "Well, Frans, here we go. Chin up and smile. That is an order!"

We hurried downstairs. He held the door open courteously and shut it behind us, and we made our way to the nearest tram stop.

No neat lines allowed passengers to file into the

trams. When a vehicle arrived, everyone pushed and shoved until you felt like a sardine in a tin. It was even more oppressive today, as the memory of those other trams returned with this pressing crowd. Daddy Long-Legs gave me a push and hoisted himself up behind me. He stood there on the platform, clinging to a pole like grim death. When our eyes met he smiled broadly, with sheer boyish fun. *"Sic mussen festhalten oder sic fallen in's wasser!"* I Shouted to him (Hold on tight or you'll fall in the water).

He roared, *Ja, Ja, Ja; ich werde aufpassen."*

It worked. Disgusted looks all around met my eyes. As people went off, my companion moved inside and stayed there till we arrived at the Central Station. It was the quickest journey I had experienced for years.

"Once we are on the train I shall not speak anymore, Frans. Don't worry about anything; just rest and relax. All will be well."

I just nodded. I hoped all would be well. If not? Well, it was a gamble. It just had to go well! The train was packed, the noise was terrible. There was adequate time to meditate and reflect, to contemplate and to wonder. Where was I going?

A slight pang of fear arose when the direction seemed unmistakably Westerborg, the central gathering camp, the last stop before final deportation abroad. But the train stopped only briefly at Westerborg, then rumbled along. Twice a Wehrmacht train packed with singing soldiers passed us. Darkness fell. The compartment was only half full of sleepy passengers. I dozed once or twice very lightly. Apprehension had not yet left me; there was the continuing underlying watchfulness which was to become my companion and second nature throughout the years that lay ahead.

Around midnight I was awakened by the train drawing sharply to a halt. I noted with amazement that we were the only two left in the compartment. Train doors opened and slammed, but my companion made no attempt to leave. Instead, he leaned forward and instructed me concerning the next step toward our goal.

"We will alight presently, but please observe silence.

We won't go near the platform. I'll help you down to the railway track. You must walk slowly and silently across the sleepers. Try to avoid the gravel; it's too noisy. I will imitate a bird's sharp night whistle and you will notice a policeman. He is all right. Don't speak to him, and once we reach the field road you will sit on the back of his bicycle. I will follow at a safe distance. Is everything clear to you? Right! Come on then, Frans, our time has come."

He opened the door, then slowly and silently disappeared below. His hands reached up for me, but I handed him my black case. Having put it down he reached up again, and I accepted the help of his strong arms. Landing quietly on my toes as instructed, I looked around. It was so dark, not a star in the sky. The air was damp; I felt shivery from lack of sleep, excitement and an empty stomach.

Holding his hand, I stepped from sleeper to sleeper. The silence was intense. Long-Legs smiled, put his fingers to his mouth and produced a beautiful imitation of a night bird's shriek. Silence! Then we heard a movement, from behind the bumpers. Suddenly, a very big broad-shouldered policeman stood right in front of us. His shiny buttons were the only light in the enveloping darkness. He lifted his hand, we stepped over the rails and followed him. In incredible silence we reached the field road behind the station and I noticed the bikes. With a gallant gesture and smile he offered me the luggage rack, so I stepped on, holding gently to his saddle. But he bent down whispering into my ear, "Put your arms around me. It's safer! We have a long, long way to go."

It certainly was a long and bumpy track. For three quarters of an hour we rode along, silently, and at a regular speed. It was a blessing that these roads were flat; hills could have proved a nightmare. Long-Legs followed at a distance with my case on his rack. The discomfort eased as I became accustomed to the bumps and bends. I was therefore almost sorry when he lowered his legs and our journey came to an end.

"Here we are," he whispered, pointing to the outline of a large square house standing somewhat off the road.

Then he informed my friend about what was to happen on Thursday night. "It's no use meeting before midnight. I would suggest 12:45 A.M. There still won't be moonlight if the clouds remain heavy. The others will meet us at the back of the Town Hall. We have had an SOS from Limburg. They need two hundred ration books, and we must concentrate on identity cards this time as well as ink pads. We only have ten minutes at the very most, but it should be sufficient. The men know their jobs; we'll just be there to supervise and ensure safety. Well, Domie, see you on Thursday then. Get some rest. Good night, good night." He slapped my shoulder and I smiled back, thanking him for all his kindness.

So, my friend's real name was Domie, short for something I supposed, or even a false name, like mine. Not having called him anything at all, I decided I would wait until I was quite sure how to address this extraordinary man.

"Don't dream now Frans, you'll soon be in bed. Come on, we'll go in by the back door. I hope you like it. This is my house." I smiled politely but tensely as we walked up the path to the house. There was not a sound to be heard. The windows were closed and shuttered; storm doors secured the front entrance.

Daddy Long-Legs tapped on the window in a strange way . . .—, . . .—, . . .—. It must be a code. It resulted in a stirring behind the door. Bolts were pulled back and forward, a key turned laboriously, twice, then two young men with grinning faces appeared with a "Hi, Domie." They greeted me with a "Hello," which I returned. Securely the door was locked behind us. Then Domie led me through the dark stone-floored lobby toward the kitchen. Light came through the cracks, someone rushed to open it wide—incredible—to subdued but delighted voices and laughter. "Oh, Domie, it's good to see you." "How are you?" "Hi, Domie."

My attention was drawn by a voice from behind all the others: "Hello, Nurse!" Was it possible? It was

Ruth, a slim young nurse everyone had given up—arrested, we had thought, during a shopping expedition.

So she was safe; as I would be from now on.

Domie, still holding me by the arm, now pushed me forward. "This is Francisca, our new member."

"Welcome, Frans," they called in turn. I smiled a thank you.

"Here, have a nice cool drink of buttermilk. You'll be ready for that by now." One of the women handed me a large mug.

"Hey, we could do with some more as well," the boys chorused. "We'll all take some more and drink Frans's health!"

"Just one moment, boys, while I introduce Frans to Aunt Jo. She'll be in the study. No buttermilk for me. . . ."

"Oxo," they chorused before Domie could finish his sentence.

Domie led me through another door into the hall proper. It was cozy here, warm, dimmed lighting and well-carpeted. There were lovely pictures on the walls, and I had a sense of security. He opened the door to the study. "Hello, my darling." He embraced his wife and they exchanged questions regarding each other's welfare, while I observed the pleasant design of the study. As their conversation grew louder I heard his wife's doubts about bringing another one. Didn't he realize the danger?

"If you only were there, my dear," he replied persuasively, "you would understand why I do it. The situation is growing worse daily, and the cruelty grows with it. We must do what we can, my dear. You must be my partner here while I work over there. We must! It is our duty and privilege." She nodded, and he stroked her head. I was worried, shy and embarrassed.

Domie turned round sharply. "Let's toast our new arrival with buttermilk and Oxo." She chuckled while we walked back to the kitchen. There, Aunt Jo put her hand on my shoulder and with a bright smile, announced: "Well, folks, Frans is our new arrival! We hope she'll be very happy with us."

The buttermilk was served and everybody was introduced to me.

The two boys, nephews of the family, were both called Dik. They were known as I and II. Both had been students at a Dutch university until the post brought them call-up papers to work for the enemy abroad. Leaving their studies to serve their country was one thing; but to work for the occupying forces—no! Immediately, they left their respective homes and went into hiding, leaving their parents truthfully unable to answer any questions regarding their whereabouts.

They had come to their uncle's residence hoping that no one would trace them so far from home. Dik I wanted to be a veterinary surgeon. He had brought many books with him to keep up with his studies. Dik II's dream was to be an architect. But I was never to see them study the subjects of their aspirations, for their voluntary duties in this unnatural life included many remote from surgery or architecture.

Then there was Lily, "the little mouse," a professional photographer from Amsterdam. She was thin, pale and very serious. Her black hair was long and straight, and hung loose around her face. It looked as lusterless as her face.

Ellie, "the big mouse," seemed more easygoing. She shook hands pleasantly.

The conversation during the introductions made me realize that these people had already been in hiding in this house for more than a year. These, then, were the mice. They occupied part of the attic. Becoming accustomed to thinking of them in this way prevented any slip of the tongue to outsiders who were totally unaware of the secret life in this house.

Ruth, the nurse who had vanished, I had known by sight at the hospital in town. She had been engaged to be married, but now was voluntarily and completely separated from her fiance.

Everyone had their own burdens, strains and tensions. Strange to say, explosions seldom occurred, I was told. There was, amazingly, much fun and laughter among this curious company.

Little mouse was the first to rise. "Excuse me, folks; I'll get on with the work." A smile passed over her usually expressionless face. The others took the hint. They too moved off, leaving their tumblers behind.

When I made attempts to clear the remains of our feast, Domie's wife stopped me.

"They'll do till after. Come and we'll have a chat in the study. We'll be in the way while they are getting ready."

Domie followed.

"Call me Aunt Jo," she began. "You will soon get used to living with the others. Ask them anything you want to know when I am not around. There are a few points you should know tonight, however, before you go to bed. We have certain safety measures which will be shown to you tomorrow. One is of primary importance to all of us. Everybody must act instantly when the buzzer goes for emergency. When you hear it once, just once, don't move! Stay where you are! Be absolutely quiet and wait for a double buzz. That is our 'all clear.' When you hear the buzzer being pressed persistently, it means danger. Follow the others! We have frequent safety drills, and you will be introduced to them in the morning. No more to burden your tired self tonight; come with me and I will show you where you'll sleep tonight. Tomorrow things will get organized."

I went over to Domie, who was partly dozing. "Good night, Domie, and thank you very much for everything; for everything!"

He sat up and replied, "Frans, it is nice to have you with us. I'll see you later."

We climbed the stairs. There was a long corridor ahead of us with doors on either side and a long full-size window at the end. With the shutters tightly closed and the black blinds drawn, we could walk in the brightness of the light which filled this house apparently everywhere.

"Come, and we'll see Bas-Jan, my baby boy. He is just eighteen months old, but, oh, so sturdy. He might be a farmer by the way he carries on in the garden each day. He won't waken. Come and see him."

He was lovely. A bundle of joy in this strange abnormal world. Would he ever talk about us once his vocabulary increased? She lifted him gently, laying him on his side, and covering him with the three little blankets which had previously looked like a ragheap entwined with toys.

"This is our room when uncle Bas is at home," she told me. "On other occasions we switch around a little for a change, with the exception of the mice. They have their permanent abode upstairs. You'll see it all tomorrow.

She turned off the light and we left quietly, crossing the passage, making for the last door on the left. It led to a small room, the smallest room in the house, I believe. Ruth and I were to sleep here that night till we got organized.

"The toilet is right at the bottom of these stairs. Now get some rest, and I hope you will sleep well."

Alone at last! Looking around, I got acquainted with the layout of my room. It was small, all right, but the bed was broad and spacious. There was a narrow table standing awkwardly alongside the same wall with the chairs neatly tucked under it. The other wall was covered by shelves of books, and at the far end there were two doors. I opened one to satisfy my curiosity. I found a small, dark, square boxroom, our "private bathroom" with a few pails, water jugs and china wash bowls—all articles carefully planned for two. Another smaller door, right opposite the double bed, I imagined, would lead to the boys' room. I curbed my curiosity.

So there I was sitting on a strange bed once more, in a strange house, among strangers, even *Goyim* (Gentiles), for the first time in so many years. The Third Reich would not allow us to mix with Gentiles but blow the Third Reich! From now on I would be illegal through and through.

I decided I had better prepare for bed as it was after 2 A.M. Quite unbelievable! The house was alive! People were moving about everywhere. The mice went back and forth, up and down, with pails, buckets, jugs and papers. Dik I and II were doing exactly the same. Ruth was on duty in the kitchen. She didn't join the activities of her colleagues. Or did she tactfully leave me to myself for a while?

Oh, how tired I was. Yawn upon yawn escaped from me, and I was hungry too. Aunt Jo wanted the cups left till later. Surely that meant they would eat once the work was done before retiring for the night?

How would I prepare for bed? I had nothing, nothing at all. I wanted to brush my teeth, but I had no toilet preparations. Oh, I was so sticky. Now to venture out—where was that toilet? Down below, near the stairs, Aunt Jo had mentioned. Well, I must have a walk, just for some exercise. The carpets felt nice and soft; it was easy to walk quietly, yet I tiptoed gently along. Halfway down, I met the big mouse. "Don't worry about the creaking staircase. You'll soon find out which steps to avoid," she laughed.

I could hear the cistern. Yes, that was the toilet. There was Domie's voice. I wanted to see him again. Without the slightest hesitation I made for the kitchen.

Ruth was preparing the food. The bread looked lovely, rather loose in texture and a bit crumbly. She cut loaf after loaf. There was butter and cheese and jam. There was also a row of tins, all shapes and sizes, and I watched her filling each to capacity. "This red one is yours, Frans; you can take it up with you later. This is our flask; we will share it for breakfast. You will get your own some day this week." So Ruth was on breakfast duty, and attended to the supper as well.

The tumblers were washed now and surrounded two heaped plates of bread. A large pot of tea was brewing, and those still busy realized that respite was at hand.

Soon we were perched on stools or sitting on chairs. They bombarded Domie with questions regarding the situation in the cities, and for news of friends and relatives. The atmosphere was quiet and serious now, and the discussion concerned the safety of all involved. They urged Domie, persistently, to take care and not to be too daring. He shook his head calmly, reassuring them.

Aunt Jo joined the company, and I learned about

the many varied projects in which these people seemed to be involved.

Little mouse was the first to rise once more. "Good night, folks. I am very tired. Good night, Frans. I'll see you in the morning. Come and see our place, will you? Good night all."

She picked up her tin and flask, and was soon followed by the others.

I helped Ruth to tidy up and was starting to follow her when Domie called me back. "Frans, may you be very happy here. Never feel lonely. We are your friends. Talk freely about anything that may worry you, and ask any questions when things seem strange to you. We are responsible for you and will do everything possible to see you through. You, in turn, will take a responsible part in the safety precautions which are of utmost importance to us all. All right?"

"I promise that, Domie." My answer conveyed utter sincerity.

"You may also call me Uncle Bas if you want. The boys do, and after all you are our youngest."

Dear Uncle Bas! I left him with a firm handshake, tears in my eyes. I was so grateful, so speechless, so tired. I wanted to go to bed, to close my eyes, to shut out everything I'd seen and heard.

Ruth was in our room when I arrived. "Here is a nightgown. I hope it fits you. Anyhow it will keep you warm. It's colder here. We are so far north."

North? I wondered. I would have loved to know where I was, but I knew, instinctively, that this was a question which must not be asked.

"This is your towel. Remember your color and keep it near your facecloth and toothbrush. We use the same soap and toothpaste, and leave it behind when we move from room to room. Down there are our pails. We keep them covered and use them when we are not allowed downstairs," that is all day until the buzzer sounds for the all-clear at night. It is very important not to use these pots when the signal for silence has gone. Absolute stillness is essential till Tantje gives us the all-clear."

I just nodded. I couldn't take in much more. Who was Tantje? Who cared? A little cat wash and I slipped into bed. Ruth watched me as I asked her which side was hers. She did not seem to mind so I chose the side next to the wall, wished her good night and closed my eyes.

Darkness, how good. Half-past three. When would the day begin in this community? Oh to sleep, to sleep, to dream, to think, to be safe!

"Almighty Invisible God of the Universe; God of Abraham, Isaac and Jacob; protect Thy people and save Thine inheritance." After reciting my Hebrew prayers for the night, I gave way to the sleep which gradually overcame me.

CHAPTER 11

When I wakened the sun was streaming into our little room. Ruth was up, the shutters folded back, allowing each ray of sunshine to penetrate. Sitting on a cushion on the floor, she leaned against the bookcase, cleaning her nails, a magazine on her knee. She wasn't aware I was awake; it gave me a chance for another respite. Closing my eyes once more I drifted into dreams and thoughts, contemplating this new existence.

How long would this war last? Would the Allied Forces win or would Germany conquer Europe and bury us alive? It couldn't be! It would be futile to hide, futile for the Resistance to fight their illegal battles, futile to retain a will to live, futile, yes, everything would be futile. The Allied Forces *had* to advance or we would be trapped like—like *real* mice.

Aunt Jo entered, and I heard her whispering voice. "Is she still asleep?" "She was stirring," Ruth replied, "but she has slipped over again. Just let her sleep this morning."

"Cheerio then, but get her up well before dinner comes up; the boys will want to get in soon."

"Right, Aunt Jo, I'll make sure she's up."

Better not open my eyes again, it would be fatal.

Time passed, how long I could not say, then Ruth moved nearer the bed. She sat down and I breathed as naturally as I could. Was she looking at me? Oh dear, I'd better stretch and groan a little.

"Sh, sh, you're all right, Frans, wake up, sh, quietly though," she whispered. "You'll soon need to get up, the dinner will be here at any time, then the boys and the mice will want to join us."

I sat up straight!

"See this window; always crawl past it, never walk upright near any windows, especially when the sun shines."

I understood. Stepping from the bed I crawled along the floor to our washroom; Ruth was still beside me. "Take your hot water bottle; you just use the water in it to wash your face. There are only the two jugs, you see, and this little glass jug for drinking only." Hesitantly, she added, "Look, Frans, you've got to use this pot during the day, then empty it into the pail, it gets emptied at night. Let me know if you have to go downstairs; I'll show you the drill."

When I opened the doors of the hidden washroom once more, Ruth had made the bed. The table now stood in front of it with chairs at either end. There was a tablecloth, but a lonely blue and white piece of corded binding puzzled me, lying there all by itself. I wouldn't ask; I would know in good time.

A quiet tap came at the door. "All right, Frans? Shall I let them in?"

"Yes," I replied.

It was 12:30 P.M. The boys entered, rubbing their hands. They chatted with Ruth. I had nothing to say. Then the mice tiptoed in and joined in the chatter. I had nothing to say once more. I just watched and listened. Would they really accept me? I would do my best and adhere strictly to safety regulations. Lily, the little mouse, announced conscientiously, "There will be a safety drill later this afternoon; it will let you know the ropes, Frans." I nodded a thank you.

Three sharp buzzes. Frightened, I looked to Ruth for guidance. Dik II jumped to his feet and disappeared.

No one seemed perturbed. Ellie sighed, "Ah, dinner!" Moments later Dik arrived back with a wooden two-tiered tray. He carried it in front of him, and it seemed heavy. What a gorgeous smell. There were serving dishes with vegetables and potatoes and a large plate with pieces of meat. There were knives, forks, spoons and corded pieces of string, all different colors.

We sat round the table. My place was on the bed beside Ruth. The plates were quietly handed round, cutlery picked up separately and laid in position, the serving dishes, serving spoons, salt and pepper placed on the table. The pudding and fruit was shifted to the top shelf of the tray. What now? We all sat ready. I just watched and waited. The boys folded their hands and bowed their heads, then all said *"eet smakelijk"* the Dutch for good appetite, and Ellie began serving the meal. Quickly I recited the Hebrew thanksgiving for this superb food. Potatoes had already reached my plate, and now vegetables and a piece of meat. Well, this was it! Mother had said I should eat, keep myself healthy and not worry about Kosher food anymore. Oh dear, how could I eat it? Dear Lord, I want to be faithful to the customs and traditions of my people. Must I eat this meat?

Lily wanted to know if I had no appetite. Of course, I had an appetite, but this meat. . . . "Don't you like meat?" she asked.

"Oh yes, I do," I assured her, "but not today if you don't mind."

"Sure we don't," they answered in chorus. Lily lifted the meat onto her plate and cut it in five little pieces. With surprise I noticed how eagerly the others swallowed their extra meat.

Now I, too, enjoyed my meal, a meal without any more snags. The gravy was delicious. I mixed it with my potatoes. I ate and listended to their newsy and strange conversation. It was so different from the normal chatter of daily life in the world of soldiers, arrests, raids and curfews.

They talked about weather forecasts, forces of wind which would allow them to grind wheat, mill their flour, bake their bread for several days ahead. Often, it seemed, no milling was possible. It was too noisy, too dangerous, since those who passed the house might hear. Then, as the bread was rationed, they needed to buy it from shops all over the district. No suspicion had to be aroused that this household needed more bread than its quota.

They talked about the British Overseas News Service. I marveled! What did they know about that?

They talked about printing papers. Whose duty was it for this afternoon? They wanted to bring me up, I suppose to the domain of our mice.

They talked about messages needed, lists to be made as Nopje was coming later tonight. We were interrupted. "Hi, Tantje," they chorused. The cheeriest-looking young girl I had seen for a long time entered our room. Her smile spread right across her face, and she broke into hearty laughter at the welcome she received.

They complimented her on the superb dinner, adding praise for other small tasks she seemed to have performed on her day off.

"Meet Frans, our latest addition," they said together.

"Yes, I've heard all about you, Frans," she beamed. "I hope you will be very happy here."

"How do you do, Tantje," I smiled and I withdrew to the bed once more. I felt so out of it all. They were so used to each other, and I didn't want to spoil their company. How would my arrival affect them all? I was determined to see that nothing hurt them, that everything should go on just the same. If they would only leave me alone, I would learn to be kind and polite and quiet and cause no one any worry or offense.

Ruth showed me the blue and white piece of cord string. "That is yours," she informed me. "Remember your colors. You use it to tie your cutlery together just as we have done." Chuckling, she added, "You must lick them clean, very clean, and scrape your plate; we use them again at teatime, they don't get washed until night, you see. We do all the family's dishes together. It saves water, unnecessary noise and time."

I tied my cutlery together as instructed. Tantje lifted

the double tray and left with a quiet "Cheerio for now."

"Well now," Ellie took the lead, "see you all at 4:30. All right? I've got things to do. Cheerio all." Lily followed.

"Come through, Frans," Dik II beckoned me, "and see our room—it will give you a glimpse of the road."

I followed the boys through the small narrow door. I had been right the previous night—that small door led to the boys' room. Oh, it was beautiful! It was a real room with carpets, dressing table, two wardrobes and the most beautiful *lits-jumeaux* I had ever seen—two single beds, joined as one with a common headboard, winged by two lockers. It was a bright room graced by colored drapes.

"It's really the spare room," they informed me. "Yours belongs to Tantje, but she shares a room with Nopje downstairs just now. We all encroach on each other's territory," Dik I remarked casually.

I nodded. There was the road. They held me back from approaching the window. I had already forgotten. There was no traffic, except a bicycle approaching. We must be right in the country. Straight across from our house was a small church, and along toward the left I noticed some activity. It was a shop, the boys confirmed. Along came a car, and we drew back a little. They smiled, "Well done, you're beginning to learn."

"Thank you for showing me your room. I will see you later. I had better get back." Once more I withdrew into the privacy of my room. My room? *Our* room!

Ruth wasn't there. The place was tidy again, and I sat down on a chair. What now? I felt sleepy again, but I had better do nothing meanwhile. Soon it would be 4:30, then I could climb the ladder to higher spheres.

Domie walked in quietly. He stayed for almost half an hour, asking questions about my home, my parents, my family, my background. He assured me that the war couldn't last much longer and that things would be normal soon.

He explained that he would need to leave home

again that evening, but would be back at midnight on Saturday. There was more work awaiting in Amsterdam.

Putting two and two together, I reckoned he would leave after his raid on the town hall, taking his catch to Amsterdam in order to supply the Resistance with ration books and identity cards. What a man!

"Good-bye, Frans, I won't see you till the weekend, be good! I trust you will settle down soon."

"Cheerio, Domie, thank you, thank you very much." He was gone. There was that church and they called him "Domie." It could, it must be, yes it must be short for *Dominee*—the Dutch word for Reverend, the minister. That meant he must be a Christian man. I had heard about nuns who grabbed Jewish children, saving them from the hands of the enemy. Then they were hidden in convents and later baptized. Oh my God, save me from such a future. Don't let me be captured by Goyim. I want to remain faithful to Thee. Rather die with my people, than live like a Goy.

No, he couldn't be one of those people. He was neither nun nor priest. He was some kind of ordinary man, no, an extraordinary man. I would trust him even if he were a dominee. After all, he would respect my faith. I had nothing to fear. Our God, after all, was the only true and living God, the God who created heaven and earth and all that dwelled therein. He couldn't and wouldn't be beaten by any false gods. He who had succeeded throughout the centuries would succeed now. My faith was strengthened, I was His by birth.

Ruth appeared once more. "Ready, Frans, the mice are awaiting to receive you!" We tiptoed along the hall and were faced by a rather frightening hole containing a ladder. "You first," I suggested to Ruth. Three smiling faces beckoned me. How on earth did they get up and down the ladder with their pails, buckets, jugs and junk? Carefully, step by step, I reached the summit, and looked around. The attic was dirty, dusty and filled with every kind of useless article. I followed them carefully through this maze, until they showed me their home proper.

Separated by rough curtaining, their sleeping quarters lay before me—plain iron bedsteads and odd feminine articles. That was all. Ellie explained, "You see, nothing but the table must remain when the danger signal goes. We must wipe out any trace of life up here within seconds, then disappear. The curtains come down and we mess up beds and other articles with newspapers and sacks. It must look as untidy as any attic does. There is some cleaning up, I can assure you, when the all-clear goes."

I understood—a little anyhow.

"It's the same down under with you and the boys. Ruth will show you the ropes, won't you, Ruth? Rule number one for us all is 'Don't spread yourselves out! Don't make yourselves at home! Be ready and able to quit in seconds.' " How easy it is to misjudge a situation. They kept this attic as uninhabitable as possible on purpose. No raid should betray a sign of habitation.

"There's not much among these beds to show you," Ellie continued, "but look among the beams." I saw nothing, but pretended I did. "See there, that's where the boys pick up Radio London. We receive true news of the progress at the front lines and the war in general. We receive secret messages, useful to our organization only. We all help to print the news we receive and some of the schoolchildren, tested and absolutely safe, take a few among their school books into town, then hand them to their appointed professor or teacher when they give their notebooks for correction. No classmate knows of the other, no one knows who is doing what. Even their parents don't know; Domie chooses his children from the Bible class. Isn't it superb?"

"What a people, tremendous, even the children!" I muttered.

"Yes, even the youngsters," Ellie continued. "You haven't met Sientje yet. She is wonderful. She works here daily, helping Aunt Jo and Tantje, and looking after the baby. She knows all about the secret life in this house, yet her parents know nothing, neither does her boyfriend. She leads the normal life of any teenager, yet inwardly she is carrying our burdens."

Lily took over. "This is the mill. Here we mill our grain when it is a good stormy day. The motor makes a horrible noise, but when it is stormy—oh boy—we do all we have in store. It sees us through for a few weeks at a time. Dik I is our baker. You should see him at work, he's wonderful. Did you taste this morning's bread?"

When I told her I had slept until dinner time, consequently missing his home baking, she chuckled with delight.

"Go and get it, we'll share it for our afternoon break. I have some jaffa juice and you supply the eats."

"Stay here just now," she added. "Wait until the boys come up; they might be willing to show you their secret transmitter."

Eventually the boys arrived, but they didn't join the female party. They began to oil their apparatus, and they swung around and behind the beams as supple as monkeys. They fetched and fixed, they carried and shifted. What and where did all this activity lead to, I wondered? Was it necessary?

"You must join our keep-fit class," Ruth suggested. "You need it and it's fun."

When I asked what form it took and when it was held, they assured me that it was open most of the day, and straightway the "five monkeys," as I termed them secretly, lined up holding onto the vertical beam, and began to swing their legs alternately in formation.

"This takes the place of a daily walk," they explained.

"But let's calm down," the big mouse advised. "We are overwhelming our baby with all that we're doing. Ruth, please get Frans's breakfast. I'll pour the jaffa juice, and we'll let Frans tell us more about life in the outside world."

Ruth went and came back, yet I had heard nothing.

We sat in the curtained mouse hole on beds, table and floor. We felt cozy, united in a common bond of illegality and separation from normal life. Their questions were endless, but I answered them as best I could, feeling one of them at last.

Domie was leaving us that night to attempt yet another rescue mission, then our life would be humdrum again, according to the long-term inmates.

"Pssstt." It was Tantje. "Early tea tonight, folks, it's *catechisatic* (confirmation class). The kids will be here at 6:30."

One by one we descended. I did not like that ladder and was glad to see the daylight in our room. What should I do now? I sat down, rose to my feet, picked up a book, sat down again, pretended to be fully immersed in its subject and thereby persuaded Ruth that I had settled at last.

Three sharp buzzes; I looked up inquiringly.

"Tea!" she said, "the boys will get it."

I nodded. They arrived with double tray, teapot and mugs. The top shelf was laden with homemade bread, butter and jam, a large piece of cheese and a pot of soup.

I wasn't hungry, but picked at my food to avoid their questions. The others chattered on. The boys discussed Aunt Jo's latest suggestion that we rise earlier each morning, keep regular hours to boost our morale, and retire earlier each night. The other agreed that Aunt Jo couldn't possibly know how we felt. Kind and good as she was, how could she realize how glorious it felt to move around the house freely? And the only time we could do that was after midnight; so we needed more sleep by day, more activity by night!

We agreed to do our best to be as quiet as possible for the sake of those who had to rise early, then we settled down for the evening. The mice retreated to their attic to do odds and ends. The boys each chose a book and I joined them. Ruth took up her sewing basket. The hours dragged on.

The doorbell rang often and loud. There were many voices—young ones—mingling with Domie's and Aunt Jo's laughter and that of the visitors. Little Bas-Janneke could be heard as well.

The others read on and I finally dropped off to sleep.

When I wakened it was dark, the shutters were closed, lights were on and the door was wide open. I could see the boys going downstairs. Ruth was also there with a bundle of washing in her arms. Domie walked in. He was dressed in the clothes I knew so well. "Cheerio all, be good, Frans. We will meet again at the weekend. I must go now or I'll miss my train."

" 'Bye, Domie," Ruth called hesitantly, "be careful!"

"Good-bye, Domie," I added, "be careful!"

We listened quietly as he ran down the stairs, waving once more. Ruth inquired if I'd slept well and if I wanted to come down with the others and help with the chores. Yes, I wanted to, very much.

My duty from now on was the care of our washroom, cupboard and toilet articles in general. It was great to feel busy once more. Ruth was still busy with the washing when I finished, so I continued with duties which I knew were ours. The others were running around with breakfast tins and flasks. I copied all I saw. Collecting our tins and flasks, I put them in the draining board in the kitchen. The flasks were rinsed and filled with water, the tins were washed out.

Time passed quickly and soon it was midnight. All work done, we gathered around the table in the roomy kitchen. Lily had been busy preparing our meal. Tea was made, the bread buttered; now we could lounge and relax. Aunt Jo came in to bid us good night. The chatter began; small talk, serious talk, gossip and news reviews, and, most important, duties to be allocated for the night.

Dinner and tea dishes had to be washed, potatoes and vegetables cleaned, breakfast prepared, flasks filled. There were delightful hours ahead of us yet!

I listened and learned. The beans would be pulled soon, and they would need cleaning and bottling for the winter months ahead. It was a big job, but Aunt Jo had a cutting machine. After cleaning and stringing them first, they were put into a small hole, a rotary handle turned and turned and out came the stringless beans, cut evenly in a huge pile. We would all take part in this operation until all the beans were securely bottled and stacked in the store. When I saw the preparation for the maintenance of our normal bodies, I marveled. There were stacks of bottles of all description. Carrots, peas, cauliflowers, cabbages, beans, cherries, gooseberries, strawberries, black currants—all gathered from this rich and fruitful land and garden. The mice had done most of the work long before the boys had come to join the working party. Several times a week a bottle was opened and savored, hence the stock had to be maintained, replenished by those foods which were in season. They talked and talked, informed and questioned me, and when 3 A.M. brought our conference to a close I was delighted to lead the way to lighter spheres.

And it was the evening and the morning of my first day.

Chapter 12

During the second night, sleep would not come. There was so much to digest. I'd seen and heard more than any book could tell. I could imagine how flat and uninteresting life must be to them, for they told me that their pig was gone. The butcher had come and silenced their beloved animal for good.

"Uh! Pig. How revolting!" However, it might be delicious, I would wait and see. We had never touched pig; it was against our religious customs and tradition. I thought, "It is funny how the different races eat foods appealing to them alone—chocolate-coated beetles, eels, oysters, pigs and hundreds of other things of whose existence I wasn't even aware."

No one had known about Rosie. She had been with them ever since she was a piglet, given to them by a local farmer who knew of their plight. Deep under the church hall they had dug a large hole or pigsty; there Rosie grew up for better or worse. She was fed, cleaned and loved day by day, or rather night by night. The hidden family and hidden Rosie became friends. Now her voice was silent and she lay buried and broken in tightly-sealed bottles.

Poor Rosie, she'd been sacrificed for many; now I

was to see the underground pigsty, our gateway to escape if the danger buzzer sounded. In this disused hole were benches, and large aluminum milk containers protecting important papers, photos and manuscripts against the perishing damp which attacked any goods left in the open.

I couldn't see it till tomorrow but they described it and told me of its origin. Once Rosie had been put to sleep the gang had started their major project, the digging of the tunnel. Pail by pail they had removed the sand, building scaffold inch by inch, shoring up walls and ceiling as the passage progressed. Dik II, as amateur architect, had sponsored the project; now the finished article might have to prove our salvation.

Tomorrow . . . tomorrow . . . at last I slept.

At ten I was wide awake, another day of care and silence. Aunt Jo brought us some mending—Bas-Jan's jackets, Domie's socks, silk stockings with big holes and ladders belonging to Tantje, Aunt Jo and Nopje—to pass the long hours.

At midday everyone gathered once more in our room to await the three buzzes which would bring the double tray and my second dinner in this secret abode—a very strange life. After our meal the hours dragged on as before. Dik I suddenly stood behind me as I stared through the curtains at the small stretch of road which could be seen from this side of the house.

"Did I give you a fright?" he smiled. "Why don't you come into our room? You could then study the road from a different angle. There isn't much to see, but you'll soon get to know the villagers and learn to recognize any strangers. One of us always has the road under observation. If any intruder should come up our drive, we can sound the buzzer, even from here, you see," and he pointed at the switch.

"Can I come with you now, then you can show me your light switch, just in case I touch it accidentally?"

"Don't you dare!" he warned me, waving his finger right in front of my nose, as he led me through the connecting door.

The shutters inside the windows had a venetian blind

effect. They were shut, which allowed us to observe the road but did not let anyone see movements inside the room. Feeling more at ease with the boys I ventured to ask some questions. Dik told me that we were far north, actually one hour's cycling distance from the German border. He encouraged me not to be frightened if I saw soldiers on the road, as they sometimes passed this way on routine patrol or on leave. When I asked him if his Uncle Bas had any connections with the church across the road, he smiled.

"He happens to be the *minister* of this parish."

Oh, so he *was* a minister! A Christian minister. He hadn't looked like one when he had kidnapped me—more like a climber, hiker or tramp. A minister! That meant he would be at home on Sundays.

Ah, well, live and let live, my Saturday would be over by then. I would keep the Sabbath quietly by myself. The other Jewish girls were certainly not orthodox. None had mentioned worship or prayer. Only the boys were not ashamed to pray in their usual way at the table.

I had always said my prayers. It came naturally, like breathing out and breathing in. I couldn't remember when I'd learned them or how small I was when taught. The worship of the Almighty Creator, the customs and traditions of our fathers, were interwoven into our homelife.

Although no prayer book was saved from our belongings, I knew enough to keep me going. On Saturday I would deliberately let them realize that I wished to be left alone during the morning hours, even if it meant praying in our washroom behind closed doors in the dark. It really did not matter as long as my heart had the right attitude. Then on Sunday I would respect *their* day of rest, and would do any job to allow *them* more freedom.

The door opened. There were the mice, followed by Ruth and a stranger. The newcomer crossed her arms over her chest, bowing deeply before us, as one doing homage, and mumbling some strange greeting. The others bowed jokingly in return. She came over to me.

"Welcome here, Frans," she said giving me a firm handshake, and I knew she meant it.

She opened her bag: to me it seemed like a party—out came toothbrushes, peppermints, newspapers, magazines, thread and elastic, a comb, a pair of suspenders, pencils, a light, shoelaces and—a box of chocolates!

"That's for you all to share around. My treat, actually from Dedde too. We had some spare coupons so we put them together and—presto—chocolates for the community."

So this was Nopje! She was like Domie in some ways, yet I couldn't put my finger on a particular aspect. I suppose being a secretary, working closely with a person day in and day out, sharing secrets such as foiling the enemy, would bring an affinity of behavior and action.

Soon after Nopje had gone, the emergency buzzer sounded. Ruth grabbed me by the arm and we slipped to our room. I watched as she hid pajamas and personal belongings behind a panel in the wall, then checked our washroom and pulled me with her down the stairs.

Avoiding the kitchen door, she opened a smaller one and signaled for me to follow. I just noticed a crop of hair disappearing. The boys! Ruth crawled on her hands and knees, quietly and quickly. There wasn't much headroom; I couldn't crawl as fast, and as my rear hit each horizontal beam of the platform overhead, I had to flatten my body even more. Relieved, I reached the hole and followed Ruth down below where she waited to close the hatch behind me. Then we joined the others in the pigsty. We looked at each other and smiled. Lily, however, pointed at her watch. "Too long," she said, "still too long. Four minutes is far too long."

"Cheer up," Dik II consoled her, "next time will be better!" There we sat and waited until the all-clear allowed us to haul ourselves through the hole, then back below the platform ceiling and out into the hall proper. We slapped and brushed each other's clothes before going to our respective domains, to spend the rest of the afternoon and evening enjoying Nopje's gifts of papers and magazines.

There were extra jobs to be done tonight since Domie would be home tomorrow for the weekend, and we wanted to do as much as possible so that Saturday night could be a family night.

The days and nights passed with monotonous regularity. One learned to sit still; to listen for the unexpected. I began to distinguish buzzer from buzzer. My nervous system was taxed, taxed beyond all endurance. Tension not known before increased daily within me. Our nights were short but peaceful, yet my mind worked overtime and drove any sleep from me. Dawn broke far too soon to another day of silence and monotony. Loneliness, fear and a modicum of self pity produced a strange effect on my weary mind.

One unforgettable night I did not join the others in the nightly chores. I was obstinate and told Ruth in no uncertain language that I *wouldn't* come down!

My throat was sore and I felt feverish all over. Aunt Jo came up and tried to reason but it was of no avail. The more she talked the more I sobbed. I could only mutter "I'm so sore, so sore, so sore."

Yes, I was sore all over, but mainly my head. I had never felt like this before; it frightened me and a vicious cycle formed.

Aunt Jo ordered me to get up and led me through the hall into her own bedroom. Bas-Jan was asleep, deep and sound as usual. "You will stay here tonight," she announced. "It's more peaceful for you and the others as well."

Peaceful or not, my pains grew worse and the tension increased. A red-hot saw seemed to be splitting my head in two, slowly but thoroughly going deeper and deeper. Often and persistently I called for a doctor.

Aunt Jo tried to explain that no doctor knew of our existence and that she could not possibly involve another person in our secret.

I couldn't understand the implications: I was sick, I needed a doctor and I would get a doctor, I had to! I ignored all her words and cried and sobbed for a doctor. Not conscious of the time that had elapsed, I was at last confronted by a stranger who called himself a doctor.

"Doctor, oh doctor," I cried, "please help me! I'm so sore, so very sore. My head, oh my head."

He held my hand, felt my pulse, examined my hot body, peered into my eyes, ears and nose, hit my knees, arms and ankles with a little hammerlike object, then gave me a long and deep injection in the leg. A relaxing sleep mastered my painful body and I was at peace.

The following night the doctor visited me again and I was calm and free from pain. Aunt Jo left us together and he explained what had happened to me. He gave me some tablets and instructions to stay in bed over the weekend. "Think it all over, my dear," he suggested. "Face facts and the situation as it stands. Accept reality but have hope in the future. You are in very good hands, in the *best* of hands. Good luck and good-bye!" He shook hands and left.

I had experienced my first migraine! It would be my companion in the years to come. I would have to learn to live with it whenever it came upon me, then pray for its departure—someday!"

Quickly I rose and tidied the bed, switched off the light and went to my room. Domie would soon be home and I didn't want him to know.

After what must have been hours, my door opened. It was Domie, with two mugs of tea on a tray. I sat up straight, tears welling up in my eyes, as I apologized sincerely for what had happened in his absence. He didn't want to hear anything about it, just emphasized repeatedly that he was sorry I had been in such distress.

Tomorrow was Sunday; he wished me a good day.

I could not imagine him in a long black gown like a minister, yet he was one. He would have to preach sermons and guide his congregation. He would have to be at many a graveside and comfort many a mourner. I supposed he would be good at that. He didn't need to say anything, he simply was comfort himself—his very being inspired courage, courage to go on.

Next morning the boys were dressed smartly. Jokingly I asked if they were going out. To my surprise, they nodded.

Evidently the Sunday morning routine followed a rigid pattern. Once the service had started, with the organ playing and the people singing their praises, the boys would tiptoe downstairs, press a clothes hanger between the connecting door and settle beside the toilet, to worship the God of their salvation, Dik I explained.

"You can come, too," he added, "Ellie sometimes comes." Politely I declined, but assured him that I would love to see Domie all dressed up.

He burst out laughing. "I'll tell him," he assured me. "I'm sure he'll come."

I'd done it! Now I would see my kidnapping tramp in holy robes. Dik was gone. I would just have to accept the result of my curiosity.

"Oh, my word, Domie," slipped out of my mouth when I saw him. He was his usual self and inquired sheepishly if he were respectable enough to go. With my very best wishes I sent him on his way.

He was a minister, a *real* one, too. I could not get over it. He looked beautiful and majestic. Those clothes made him look even taller. His narrow face and thin hair seemed unequal to command all that there was of him; yet his eyes and his very personality spoke of a greatness with which he walked hand in hand, a phenomenon difficult to define yet powerful in experience.

I could hear the first hymn—men, women and children's voices mingling. The boys would be sitting beside the toilet mouthing the words without a single sound. The services were usually held in the church, but between mid-September and mid-April the church could not be heated sufficiently to draw the villagers from their home fires, hence this special arrangement. The boys liked it, as it enabled them to go to church.

The hour passed quickly and the boys had to disappear before the worship ceased. We all sat together on the bed and watched those smartly-dressed farmers and their families leaving the drive by bicycle or on foot.

Dinner was later on Sundays, but when the familiar two-tier tray arrived, it was worth waiting for. There was a three-course dinner; fruit, soup, cabbage, meat and an extra piece of fat to mix with the potatoes.

One had to be very tactful and polite to decline such delicacies as pork with its fat. Tantje had noticed; now she always sent some extra gravy or a little butter to moisten my potatoes.

There truly was a different atmosphere within the house on a Sunday. Would it be like that each week?

The afternoon was spent lazily: reading, musing, sleeping, we were free as usual till the hour of darkness. Free, but compelled to be extra silent. Visitors, callers, even children loved to come and go freely on Sundays. This had to continue or suspicion might be aroused.

After tea we continued in quietness and idleness. Sunday was the longest day of the week; it was most trying mentally as well as physically. We never saw Domie after tea. He spent some time with his wife and son as well as time alone in meditation before the evening service. Then, when the last amen rang through the hall, Domie would walk calmly and reverently from his pulpit, through the connecting door and disappear into his study. Aunt Jo awaited him, helped him to change and be out of the house in his old clothes and onto his bicycle in record time, even before the organ had quieted and the first parishioners had left the building.

With gathering speed he cycled toward the station three-quarters of an hour away and just managed to catch the last train to one of the large cities, to seek and to save the lost—lost among thousands of others being herded into trains, lorries, camps and gas ovens.

He would mingle with the crowd, pass his messages to Resistance workers who moved about just as freely as he did, and receive reports regarding the special desperate few.

We were among the few and we had to be patient, to

endure the *isolation*, instead of the *desperation* among the doomed milling crowds. We all had to face up to whatever lay before us.

A new week lay ahead, yet all were alike. Did we really look for variety? Monotony surely was better than the variety which we had known so well in the days gone by. Yet there was variety even amongst the most sleepy monotony.

I remember one morning the danger signal buzzed in all of our rooms. Fortunately it was around ten-thirty in the morning and we had risen, tidied the beds and eaten our breakfast.

My tongue was frozen to the roof of my mouth, and I was shaking at the knees. I checked that none of my night attire was lying around, then raced down the stairs, and, being the last, Tantje shut the connecting door behind me. Crawling on my hands and knees I soon reached the hatch which gave access to our underground passage.

It was a full half hour, to us an eternity, before the all-clear sounded throughout the house and in our secret passage. Voices and steps came nearer, but still we did not make a move. In all our minds was one thought, one thought only: had he or they, whoever they were, discovered the buzzer and forced Aunt Jo to divulge the correct signal to get us out without resistance?

The steps were right above us now; it could not be army boots. Then Tantje's voice: "Are you still there?" followed by her usual chuckle.

Dik I made the move. He sped to the hatch door and pushed, while Tantje pulled it open. Dik helped each of us out and followed last, covering our opening until the next time.

Tantje was bombarded with questions.

"Get upstairs now," she urged, "I'll be up in five minutes with some hot coffee and then you'll get the whole story."

We settled down on the large bed in the boys' room, where Aunt Jo joined us, smiling as usual but strangely white around her nose and forehead.

"Well, that's over!" she said calmly. Tantje arrived with the coffee and between them they told us what had happened.

Two German soldiers had marched up the drive after their car had suddenly screeched to a halt. The noise had alerted Aune Jo and, as she saw them jumping from the vehicle, she had given the alarm signal for us to disappear. The soldiers had rung politely at the front door and asked if they could come in!

Shyly and slowly they began their story. A nice young Dutch girl at the border had been friendly with the younger soldier for some time. Could Domie marry the couple in a religious ceremony in the church or in his vestry? The soldier had friends in his battalion whom he could bring to the manse as witnesses!

CHAPTER 13

Once most of the extra autumn work of bottling vegetables was done, we all began to prepare for St. Nicholas Day, on December 5. Handmade presents for everyone in the house were placed in a large hamper, and the boys made up humorous songs and poems for us to sing and recite.

After the celebration of that Dutch holiday, the others began to prepare for Christmas. Christmas, connected with church and worship, they assured me, would be more serene and joyful. We could even feel some of that here in our own quarter.

Since I had gone into hiding, I was unsure of the true dates of my own Jewish festivals, so I decided to observe them with the Christian festivals. While they prepared for Christmas, I prepared my heart and imagination for Hanukkah.

Last year we had celebrated Hanukkah at home. I was in bed with scarlet fever. My parents received my gifts with the words, "God with us." Where were they today? "Oh, God, be with them as Thou has promised of old," I prayed.

Yes, I would celebrate Hanukkah in my heart, I was determined. Aunt Jo's Christmas lights would be my

Hanukkah lights. No one would see the worship of my heart to the God of my fathers. If only I had my Hebrew Prayer Book, my Old Testament Scriptures. But who was able to take such risky items on a flight into hiding?

I thought of poor Joseph. His jealous brothers deceived their father and sold the lad to strangers, who took him to a far country. He must have been terribly frightened down in that deep pit all alone, before he was brought up and given to those men of a different nationality and custom. How cruel can one's own flesh and blood be? Yet, see how kind and helpful Joseph turned out to be when those selfsame brothers were near to starvation. That's how I imagined God would be someday. He would forgive and accept His wayward family. Joseph was like Moses, a man who remained faithful to the God of his fathers, although far removed from all religious influence.

Hidden away in strange premises, separated from all childhood customs and observances, I would be like Joseph, yes, I would! After all, God is so mighty and understanding He would see my heart's devotion and surround me with the same love He had shown to my forefathers.

Aunt Jo had written an outline for the Christmas service. She asked if our printing machine could make a hundred copies or more and if we all would get busy stapling the sheets. We did this that same afternoon. They looked very pretty. Young Dik had sketched some twigs, stars and flowers here and there on the front page. One looked almost like a *Magen David* (Star of David). I asked to shade those twigs with green ink and give a touch of color to each service sheet. They were as delighted with the suggestion as I was with this extra piece of work.

They were Christian hymns, but some had the word "Israel" in the verse, which greatly surprised me and made me wonder just where the connection could be. I thought it strange to see Almighty God as the focus of their worship, their prayer, all in straightforward Dutch.

The second page of the program had a story—their Christmas story. Glancing over the lines, I noticed that the Jews came into it as well and once more I was certain that these Christians must know more about us than we gave them credit for.

Christmas came and went, but we, the secret occupants of that house, knew little of what it meant to those who were free. Ours was a royal share of the Christmas fare, but that was all.

Nineteen forty-four made its entry quietly. We welcomed it with heavy hearts. What would the future hold for us in these coming months? We approached them as always on a day-to-day basis.

It seemed as if those early weeks in January were like a very slow motion film—no encouraging news from the front lines, no ray of hope for our people, no break in the constant arrests which continued around the clock in all parts of the country. "Patience and courage" was our motto for 1944.

That year did not bless us with the good weather everyone had hoped for. It depressed our spirits and made us wonder if the war would ever end.

Among the hundreds of books lining the walls of almost every room, I found a beautiful, color-illustrated children's Bible. Was it childish to delve into history, a history which fed an inward faith in the invisible Creator of the universe? These stories were so familiar, interwoven in my very being from an early age. Yet they were far more full of meaning at the age of eighteen, and in these surroundings, than during my primary school days. I knew myself to be part of the people with whom God had dealt from century to century. Throughout my reading it became clear to my conscience that it was essential for man's peace and security to follow God's plan of living.

A great awe for the God of our fathers stirred in my soul; workship had a new form and meaning as day succeeded day. I realized that I could worship without words or prayer book. My inner self knew it had been accepted by this eternal Being, resulting in almost childlike contentment and happiness amidst sordid captivity and inhibitions.

Certain passages of the prophets' exhortations and their condemnations were totally unfamiliar to me. They were my "Latest News" and more important to my daily diet than the BBC broadcast of front-line progress. What outspoken characters those often lonely men of God were! They cared not for personal danger as long as God's will was proclaimed. A general theme was common to all; God would one day send the Messiah. He would deliver Israel and call nations to see true light in God, discovering the eternal purposes for mankind as a whole.

Why had I previously been so totally unaware of all these personalities? Why were these stories and important events so obviously connected with all I knew from childhood? And why did these Christians have a Bible on their bookshelves which dealt with my people?

"Oh my God, I wish You could answer all my questions with the voice of a human being. You are in hiding as much as we are," I used to think.

One person outshone all others in these stories—a new prophet born in Israel. Some called Him Lord, others Master, some Messiah. He was also laughed at and even rejected like all prophets before Him. Men of God had to face hardship sooner or later. I liked this One, this Stranger to me. He was more realistic, not so square as the older ones who had lived before His time. He seemed to be "with it" in many ways. In other respects He was as steadfast as a rock, even speaking out to those in authority when another would have flinched and tried to be tactful in order not to offend. He was honest, thorough and fearless even in the face of the fiercest opposition.

He was born in strange circumstances. Strange indeed and yet, why should anything be strange or miraculous if God is behind a situation, for then a strange incident becomes the most natural happening on earth.

He was unusual. He called God "His Father." So did I of course, but He acted on that relationship and was as close to Him in effect as I was to my father when we were still together.

His relationship and worship were less traditional than I had known it; His outlook and behavior to God more up-to-date. Although a Jew like myself, He practiced His faith in an unorthodox manner, yet it impressed those around Him more than the traditional way of the fathers.

Some wanted to learn from Him and follow Him. First He dissuaded them, then began to call some to come with Him—almost like a command—first two, then four and so on. They just left everything in their homes and even their daily work to obey His compelling command. Inwardly my spirit was deeply moved. He preached new and strange things regarding the approach to Almighty God. He drew attention to the fact that He was the Way, the Truth and the Life and that no one could come to the Father but by Him. That was tough meat to digest. I did not feel He should have made such high and mighty statements as that. It somehow lifted Him above all previous prophets. But then, if He *were* that promised Messiah, He had every right to speak like that! If so, we should accept and worship Him as such. No, He couldn't be. If He were, why was the world in such a mess now? But if He were *not* the Messiah, who on earth was He? He definitely was Somebody special and Someone secret, too, because no one had ever told me about Him.

As the weeks and months passed by, His life became part of mine. The readings about Him and incidents concerning Him became more important to me than anything else in my own environment. I found I could tolerate my isolation without frustration, always longing for the next opportunity to learn more about Him, for He had become my hero.

One Sunday morning in February I carefully inquired of the boys what drill was necessary for the Sunday morning visit to the space between toilet and the church hall. They advised me to bring blanket and hot-water bottle, and to follow them when they gave me the signal. That morning I listened to my first sermon. Uncle Bas spoke loud and clear. His voice inspired me with more awe and reverence for him than ever before. He read from John 13 and elaborated on the service aspect of Christ's ministry and the lesson it should be to any who were contemplating throwing their lot in with His. "You call me Master and Lord? You say well, for so I am, if I then have washed your feet you also ought to wash one another's feet! In short, I have given you an example, that you should likewise. The servant is not greater than his Lord. Happy are you if you understand this, know these things and do them." (*see* 13-16).

"No," Uncle Bas said, "it does not lie in the washing of feet only. Service to your fellowmen must cover every aspect of life; carry each other's burdens and so fulfill the law of Christ.

"If you had lived in His day and bicycles had existed, all of you here would have been pleasantly surprised because after worship you might have seen Jesus Christ in the shed behind the church hall, finishing the blowing up of your tires!"

I enjoyed the company of my Bible and my newfound prophet and hero, Jesus. At times, unwillingly, I realized that the Christians also knew someone called Jesus, but I rejected the possibility that it could be the same one as my Jesus. Grudgingly protecting Him from heathen claims, I crowned Him with Jewish glory.

Why did my people not talk about Him and learn from Him? It would have done them so much good. I had to find out more about this once the war was over.

The events of His life progressed in a most extraordinary way. Was it a story, a play or reality? He got Himself into awkward places and situations, actually refusing the easy way out and saying that He had come into the world for a purpose and that purpose was to die finally like a criminal. He came to overcome death with life.

I felt that Jesus, who lived centuries ago, had, in some unexplainable way, taken an interest in me with a loving touch. Although we couldn't see each other or communicate as human to human, deep in my heart I was assured of His victory over the cross. While still reading of His agonies, I wished for Him to show the power that was His, to free Himself from that cross.

It was a puzzle! I was too baffled by all I had read, by my deep disappointment and by the unexplained behavior and defeat on the cross. Now all was lost to me. Secretly I treasured a dead, unreal hope, clinging desperately to its memory, mourning Him who had for days been my shining example of love.

According to the custom of my people I mourned for Him for seven days. I abstained from all but the necessary food. I banned all reading from my daily routine. My thoughts were wholly centered on my loss and a deep sense of depression settled upon me. I was weepy, edgy, moody and unhappy.

None of the others knew of my personal loss, my great grief, hence I was watched with deep concern. This irritated me considerably. After seven days, according to the law, I gradually returned to normal work. Although still full of a tragedy, which had impressed me more than I dared to admit to myself, I endeavored to appear careless and lighthearted. We were so linked up with each other that the most frustrating atmosphere developed when one or the other of us stopped talking for a day or two. It did happen and we learned to live with it, but it created a divided group spirit. "What's the matter?" was a frequent question. If the person wanted to talk all would be well pretty soon. If, on the other hand, a constraining silence lay on a burdened heart or mind, if he or she just couldn't speak about it, the situation would be more serious and drag on for days.

At that time I created such an atmosphere. How could I even have tried to explain to anyone all that had impressed itself on my mind over the past few weeks? The situation had to be worked out slowly and thoughtfully. I was determined to find out why the family which gave us such generous hospitality harbored these books and others like them. Of course, Domie was a clergyman, a Christian clergyman, but what had this to do with our Scriptures being in his home? And then the story about this unknown Jewish prophet called Jesus. What a mystery it all was! I'd even found a black book which clearly contained all of our Pentateuch, our Psalms, our major and minor prophecies, yet there was something different about it. There was not a Hebrew word to be found anywhere—Hebrew letters yes, but just a few, for example, in Psalms 119. There were also many books I'd never heard of.

This section, at the back of our Bible, was separated from the rest by a blank page, followed by an introductory notice which read "The New Testament of our Lord and Saviour Jesus Christ."

Jesus Christ! There it was again! The same name as I had found in the children's Bible. Here was the same story in biblical, old-fashioned language.

It must be a special religion, I thought, a leaning toward the Jewish faith, hence their kindness in taking us in. I forced myself to shut my mind to all those deliberately trying to reject all these writings which were so very confusing. The days passed by occupied in the usual way. Slowly I came to a halt in my discoveries, outwardly indifferent and almost the same inwardly. If only my feminine curiosity would bring me the true peace I longed for. There was an underlying unsatisfied urge to find out more from either that black book or the children's Bible.

During waking hours and during the hours of darkness, when sewing, sunbathing, eating or washing up, my thoughts dwelt on the unfinished subject. My craving had to be satisfied. I would read once more the chapter of my personal loss and then continue with the story of what had happened after His death.

Again I looked at the colored picture with the three crosses; I studied His face and those who stood near. The whole event was alive once more as it had been some ten days ago. "Now I know that You couldn't come down from that cross," my thoughts silently told Him. "It was crude and cruel to do such a thing to You, because You were good, kind and somehow different from Your predecessors. Had I been with You throughout Your travels, I would have stood by You. I wouldn't have let anyone touch You, Lord. If they had only listened to me, I would have drunk Your bitter cup for You. You didn't deserve it, Lord." Why did I call Him Lord? It was strange; but it didn't matter, my ears didn't hear what my heart reasoned. My mouth would surely refrain from such audible statements.

Back I went to history and its unfolding. With a deep sigh, I settled down to read chapter 20 of this unfamiliar book called St. John.

It was now the first day of the week and Mary went back to the sepulcher with spices. She was determined to anoint the body of Him who had been so understanding to her and so considerately kind at all times. They would preserve His dear body as long as possible, foiling the attacking element which sought to reduce all matter to dust and ashes.

Deep in thought and with sorrowful countenance, she walked steadily to the place where He had been left on Friday. Then she saw the stone had been rolled away from the opening.

What could have happened? Excitedly she ran ahead. When her eyes had grown accustomed to the twilight in the tomb she shuddered with fear and sudden shock: the place was empty! What next? Numb and weary, Mary stumbled into the bright morning light. What could she do? Who could have been so crude, so disrespectful, as to assault the body of Him who only came to bless, to do good and point men to the only hope in life and death. Yes, it was true, He had made enemies in His lifetime. His purity had uncovered all wickedness, all hypocrisy. No one could hide his true motives under a cover of godliness. He saw through it all. His eyes would pierce one's very contemplation of evildoing, would make one halt with sheer shame.

Were His enemies no longer frightened, now that He lay still and cold? Did they want to destroy any bodily memory? Why had God Almighty never interfered? He surely lived close to Him and was obedient to His will. Had He not earlier, during His service to God and man, been confirmed with the words: "This is my beloved Son in Whom I am well pleased, hear ye Him." How then had God allowed this atrocity to scandalize the image of the dead?

Having fought back her tears for so long, Mary now gave way to her grief. She felt as I had done during these past ten days, and again I joined in her sorrow.

Incredibly, the story took a remarkable turn. Someone had come near to Mary and had spoken these words, "Woman, why do you weep so bitterly; whom are you looking for?"

Not interested in the identity of the kind gardener, she replied, probably without looking at him, "They have taken away my Lord and I don't know where they have laid Him!"

Almost unaware of the brief pause in conversation, she was startled when the same voice called her name, reassuringly, lovingly: "Mary."

When her eyes met those of Him who had uttered her name, she knew with indisputable certainty. "Master!" Surprised and delighted she fell at His feet, longing to kiss His blessed hand once again.

Gently He evaded her. "Don't touch me yet," He said, "but go into Galilee and tell my people what you have seen and heard. I will meet them there."

"Master!" Dropping her spices and balm, Mary hurriedly left, exuberant and radiant with joy.

Joy! Didn't I know how she felt! I could have jumped with the thrill I experienced, but I had to be so quiet. I knew it, I knew it, I'd known it all along! Death would not be able to triumph over Him. He was a true Prophet of the Most High, and favored by God above all who had gone before Him.

Lifting my heart to God I prayed that He would raise up someone like this Jesus today, one who could perform miracles and deliver us from all this persecution and discrimination. It had been a story with a truly happy ending. I read on, delighted with the miraculous change in events.

The incidents took place in a clear and precise manner, easy to understand, yet puzzling in reality.

Why had I never been told about his part of our history? It clearly was a historic event, yet it never had been mentioned during my junior or senior education.

I had to find out and I would!

During the next forty days this living Prophet showed Himself to many, still teaching, still pointing people to God and talking about His future; about His invisible reign through the Spirit once He had left the earth. He told those standing around too, that He would "return in like manner."

That was that!

From now onwards one read how He worked through all those lives which allowed Him to use them, as a tool. This was pictured in a very realistic way.

Then my favorite portion began. It taught me more than almost anything I had learned previously. It spoke of an orthodox Jew, a rabbi. He, too, was confronted, like myself, with the new Prophet and His claim of Messiah. He had never met Him, but had heard all about Him and believed that it was a hoax, someone blasphemously claiming to be sent from God. He would fight for the faith of his fathers: the preservation of the truth: the one Eternal God. There was born one who was to fight a holy war, one whose aim was to destroy those who called themselves Christians. Permission to do this was granted to him and letters of introduction to synagogues in other parts of the country were safely tucked away in his leather pouch.

As he journeyed along thinking about the ridiculous situation to which his people had succumbed, he heard his name being called. Repeatedly he looked at his fellow travelers, who in turn wondered about their leader's behavior. Who then was calling his name? Hesitantly he ventured to talk to apparently no one. "Who art Thou, Lord?" The answer was the severest blow the young rabbi had encountered during his professional career. "I am that Jesus, whom you are persecuting."

He could not see anyone. All of a sudden his eyes were blinded. His fellow companions didn't quite know how to console or calm him. He wanted to be alone to think. He had been humiliated and defeated by the very Prophet he sought to destroy.

When he arrived at his destination, he was a different man. The new believers there were frightened of him, knowing his reputation. They feared a strange trick when he wanted to join them. Those who had been awaiting him were also at a loss, for instead of denouncing this apostle Jesus, he uplifted Him in all his conversation and humbly acknowledged His living personality, telling everyone about his extraordinary experience on the Damascus Road.

Yes, it was a moving and realistic story and according to these writings this Jesus was alive, living again through the lives of those who allowed Him to use them.

A beautiful account, but not of much use for me or my people who were hunted from generation to generation. Why did Almighty God allow all this hardship, suffering and death? Where was the answer?

CHAPTER 14

I had read a lot in the past few weeks. It had kept me quiet and probably widened my outlook. The daily monotony took over once more. We heard horrible reports from the cities. Arrests and atrocities continued and we were tired of waiting for the end.

Domie hardly came home now. He was suspected of illegal activity. Rumors had to be taken seriously; one could not afford to take a risk. Sometimes he came after dark for a brief spell with his wife, to bring us news, or to help us with any trouble that had to be faced. Long before sunrise he would be gone, once more on his way through the high cornfields opposite the manse, his trusted territory. If the enemy were near, the corn would protect and afford a means of escape.

His visits became fewer and fewer. The strain, tension and worry increased each day. The manse was under suspicion. Quick action was called for.

One night in April, 1944, when we were assembled in the kitchen, we heard his familiar knock at our back door. We sensed at once that something important was afoot and we called Aunt Jo.

Domie told us that orders had been circulated for his

arrest. The manse might be searched. We all had to leave. Accommodation for each one of us had been arranged, and our exodus would begin at midnight tomorrow. What we had feared so long had come to pass.

Each one dwelt on his own position. We had to wait and see what was planned for us. Our lives were in their hands. Quietly we went through the evening routine, only more thoroughly than usual. All possible clues had to be destroyed. We packed a few personal toilet articles and went to bed.

The next day was unusually burdensome. It was the last time we were ever all together.

"Oh, for a Jesus Christ today," I thought. If ever I needed assurance regarding the living God, it was that day. That night we were to be taken to an unknown destination. I needed Him to give me courage; I coveted deeply. His assurance of protection.

The two boys were very composed. They went about their daily tasks quietly. After an early evening meal Aunt Jo asked us to get dressed and bring to the dining room all we intended to take with us. All that I had fitted comfortably into my little black case. Clothing was unimportant. My body could take care of that. I wore several pairs of stockings and socks, a few sets of underwear, dress, skirt, pullover, jacket and coat. Walking was rather a cumbersome job, but all these things had to be taken care of and would be necessary if I reached my new home.

Aunt Jo had settled herself at the piano. She played her own church songs. The boys sang tonight and so did she. We girls listened and some of us followed the words in the little songbook. Personally, I wouldn't have minded singing some of them, if only that name Jesus Christ hadn't appeared on practically every page. I couldn't bring myself to pronounce it. A solution was easily found. I *did* sing! Once I got the tune I began to sing, but all honor ascribed to Jesus, I, in turn, passed on to Moses! Whenever they assured their Lord and Master of implicit childlike trust in times of danger, I assured Moses of the strength I gained from his fine example and service to God and man. "What a friend we have in Jesus" became "What a friend we have in Moses."

This singing session was the nearest I had known to normal life for more than a year. It passed the time through the hours of dusk till we all had to leave and it lifted the strain from our heavily-taxed shoulders.

They came for me first. I shook hands with everyone, thanked Aunt Jo and Tantje for all they had done, and waddled out of the room. Aunt Jo saw me to the back door and asked if there was anything else I needed. I had hoped she would ask me. There was no other way to tell her. Rather shyly I asked if she would allow me to take the little black book from upstairs with all the Bible stories, and if she could spare it, one of the songbooks we had used that night. Not at all surprised, she consented and asked me to wait a moment while she fetched them. It was the first time I had openly mentioned the strange book.

The police officer had arrived; it was time to leave. Could it be imagination or was Aunt Jo's kiss warmer this time? While passing through the dark garden I picked a pansy and slipped it carefully into my book. I treasure it to this very day, pressed among the pages of my little black book.

As when I arrived, so now, I traveled on the back of a bicycle. The journey was almost as long, and just as uncomfortable, although I was more padded than on the previous occasion! Our journey ended before a row of gray stone laborer's cottages. The police officer rang the bell of one of the houses. The door was opened, but no one could be seen or heard. No words were exchanged, but an arm stretched out and pulled me inside. Once the door was shut and bolted, a voice whispered, "Sorry, no light, my dear, no one must know you've come, you see."

It was a relief to know that the ordeal had passed so quickly and without incident. The lady was kind and informed me that they had one other illegal person in their home. I would have to share the bed inside the wall cupboard. The doors were opened at night but closed during the day. As at the manse, we were only allowed to move at night, but more care had to be observed in this new abode. A ladder from the hall led through a skylight to the attic. We climbed this ladder early each morning before the sitting-room curtains could be opened and the blackout removed. The hatch was then closed and we had to endure silence till the hatch opened for the delivery of meals or for an occasional chat, if no visitors were expected.

A pail with lid provided for our personal needs up there. Did my new landlady wonder why a broad smile spread over my face? I gloried in the promotion to a "Pail-and-lid mouse"; now I had the status of the "manse mice." Where are they? I wondered. As I began to drift dreamily along this line of thought I must have missed some of the instructions. However, I was soon brought back to reality as she prepared to introduce me to my bedmate and fellow diver, as we illegals were conveniently called.

She led me to the little sitting room at the front of the house, opened the door and there standing beside the table in this small room, was Sister Moony—a department Sister of our Amsterdam hospital, dreaded by most juniors!

Sister Moony! No, I needed no introduction. We knew each other too well and this meeting took me entirely by surprise. Smiling faintly she shook my hand. I, in turn, felt it my duty to reciprocate by producing a faint smile as well.

Once this formal, unnecessary introduction was over, I waited automatically till she offered me a seat. A duty atmosphere was in existence!

My new landlady, who introduced herself as Tantje's sister, brought each of us a mug of hot chocolate and some biscuits. Then it was time to prepare for bed. Sister Moony led the way. At night we were permitted to use the kitchen for washing. I followed wherever she led me—ultimately to bed.

Bed was the cupboard behind the doors which I had seen previously. The mattress was held firmly between the wall and an outer horizontal plank. The bed was immaculate and I was invited to get in first. Sister

Moony pushed a chair near the doors and I began my journey onto the chair—over the plank, and on the creaking bed—rubbing the soles of my feet against each other to lose the last speck of dust before partly disappearing under the blankets on my side of the bed.

Sister Moony—in bed with me! The nurses' home in the hospital would have been spilt wide open with hilarious laughter, but I felt no such temptation. On the contrary, as soon as my head touched the pillow, I crossed my ankles and folded my arms. Sister made herself comfortable and insisted I move over another two inches. Now my left side rested against the wall. Pulling the blanket over that shoulder I began to contemplate this new situation, but my mind soon went blank, and I slept the sleep of exhaustion.

Next morning Sister Moony wakened me with tea and bread which I consumed as soon as I managed to sit upright. Still feeling sleepy, I was in no mood for conversation. This suited the boss who began instructions to her junior. I must rise as soon as I had finished my tea, make the bed, close the doors, wash in the kitchen and follow her to the attic.

Doing as I had been instructed, I soon reached a tiny room among the thick beams. This quick ascent was greeted with a smile of approval. The ladder was removed, the latch closed and we settled down to quietness till the hour of release, at sunset.

Downstairs the husband began to pull up all blinds, open the windows and doors, answer the milkman and baker. No one suspected that up in the attic two human beings were awaiting a favorable end to the war. I was sad and unhappy in my new surroundings. It was exasperating to have Moony around me all day, and probably she felt the same about me. It is difficult to learn the lesson of forebearance and patience!

We saw our landlady only three times each day—halfway through the morning, when she opened the hatch and handed us potatoes and vegetables to clean, lunchtime, and in the afternoon, if the house were free, to hand up a cup of tea.

The rest of the day I was under Moony's authority.

Every morning after we had settled down for the day there was a short lecture on the benefit of healthy bodies in times of physical restraint. These bodies had to be excercised to keep them supple, fit and healthy. She would show me what to do. Then I began to realize why we didn't get fully dressed downstairs: gymnastics was her ever-important theme.

It must have been funny—both of us marching round behind one another in stocking soles and underskirts! Moony's hair hung down her back and swung to and fro with every jerky movement. Whether I felt like it or not, I had to follow Moony around that attic, morning after morning.

During the long hours of each day I often tried to make conversation, but soon realized that there, too, I was an intruder. She was interested in conversation only when she could tell me what to do! We developed our own mode of life.

No news of the war reached us. We depended on what the enemy broadcasts stated or explained. We only existed. I became dull and very passive. The manse life had been more active, especially in the evenings. The mice and the boys would discuss matters of interest and I could listen and learn, while Nopje and Tantje popped in and out with news, humor, or just a cup of tea. This was like solitary confinement, as my companion was not interested in my presence; indeed she resented this intrusion into her haven of safety and quiet. She didn't want cheering up, conversation or discussion. We lived, ate and slept together, yet we were miles apart.

I turned again to the God of my fathers and began to read my little black book. I made no effort to hide my interest and her presence did not worry me. The attic became my cloister. I learned more during my brief stay there than I did anywhere else in the years that lay ahead.

The Psalms, the Kings and Prophets and once more the New Testament thrilled me. It seemed strange that all the stories of the Children's Bible were in this little book as well as our old Scriptures. They fitted in and I delighted to read them. In the fifth Book of Moses, chapter eighteen, verse fifteen, Moses talked of a new prophet to rise from amidst the nation. He should be heard and obeyed. To me this was none other than this outstanding Person, this Jesus Christ, born into our nation, one of our kith and kin, brought up in the law and prophets. He spoke with authority and full knowledge of our history, our backsliding, our means of return and restoration.

The attic room we occupied in this gray stone house was small but attractively furnished and decorated. While the mice in the manse had only the bare essentials, we enjoyed a splash of color in furnishings and decoration. Instead of the actual countryside, we could look at pictures representing the finest scenery of a free country. When continual sitting became tedious and a strain, a divan along one wall allowed us to stretch out. Mrs. Goody cared for us with true concern and love. Our meals were wholesome and nourishing; nothing was lacking except our freedom.

Days and weeks dragged by. Horrified, I discovered that all gladness had drained from me. Would I ever know how to laugh again? Laughter hadn't been in evidence for many months. It was dangerous from the noise point of view, and indeed what cause for laughter could be found in such monotonous conditions? To think that I had ceased to be glad, I who had to be constantly checked by teacher and parents alike for my happy-go-lucky way of living; I had forgotten how to laugh! This realization frequently brought tears to my eyes. It made me even sadder and lonelier than before. "Whom have I in heaven beside Thee and who is there in earth whom I would desire above Thee," was the deep cry of my heart.

More and more my thoughts turned to the God of the impossible. He was explained and portrayed so clearly by this prophet Jesus Christ, that I almost felt that I knew Him—that I could depend on Him—that I could take Him at His word and live according to His advice. It only worried me when this Jesus Christ made definite claims regarding His purpose on earth or His authority; or proclaimed His apparent divinity and the part He played in our approach to the Almighty Creator of the Universe. Some of His own words would come to me:

> No man cometh unto the Father, but by Me.
> I am the Way, the Truth, and the Life.
> Come unto Me . . . and I will give you rest.
> All power is given to Me in heaven and in earth.
> I am come that they might have life.

Unconsciously, He had stolen His way into my life, and I could no more think of God the Father without visualizing Jesus Christ. Slowly but surely, God became a reality in my thoughts. I learned to consider Him; weighing my actions and aims as they would affect Him and His cause.

As day succeeded day He must have drawn me closer and closer to His heart, for my Scriptures were a constant oasis in this perplexing and frustrating desert of underground existence. The New Testament became to me a more and more up-to-date account with a similarity to events which were taking place in our own age. I could imagine Domie, Aunt Jo, Tantje, Nopje and Sietje as disciples of Jesus Christ.

The thing which never ceased to baffle my questioning mind was the strange phenomenon that all the people I knew who followed Him were not Jewish at all, and had no apparent connection with Judaism, its religion or tradition—they were Gentiles of all nations, yet they prayed to the God of Abram, Isaac and Jacob. They sang the psalms of David and read the prophecies and were interested in Israel as a country. If they left this Prophet and His name out of their prayers and songs, they could be Jews of a high and sincere status, and could be instructed in our rituals and dietary laws and strengthen our ranks beneficially.

As it was, the whole scene appeared upside down. The Gentiles used our Holy Writ, learned from our prophets, worshipped Almighty God and His messengers, and yet—they were not Hebrews.

If these war days taught me anything worthwhile, it was the true biblical history of my people, their aspirations and hopes, their longing for God's revelation in a Messiah of His choice.

A plaque above the door in our little attic attracted me. The message was true, as if the dead thing knew me through and through, "man looketh on the outward appearance, but the Lord looketh on the heart" (1 Samuel 16:7). So true! Neither Sister Moony, nor anyone else, knew my heart, my searchings, my contemplations; they all saw the outward appearance—only God knew my heart!

A vital truth surged through my very being—death and—life! He's alive! He worked and pleaded still with humanity, it was He who had been busy with me all these months. His vast almighty and penetrating Holy Spirit had pierced my iron curtain of reasoning.

"*Rabboni,* Master, *my* Master and my God!" A supreme sense of absolute safety and belonging filled my excited and happy being. Within seconds, meaning, purpose and security presented itself to my reason. There was hope for this world, hope through this unknown Saviour, this Jesus Christ.

To the amazement of Sister Moony, I left my potatoes half peeled, laid down my knife, rose from my stool and without an explanation left the little room. Outside among the attic beams and in a little corner of the roof, I slowly knelt down, clasped my hands in absolute surrender and closed my eyes to all around.

"*Rabboni Joshua Hamoschiach,* Master Jesus Christ!" It was all I could whisper. Deep thankfulness and love to Almighty God for His inexplicable revelation and gift flooded my entire being. God cared! He cared after all! He was interested in His people!

If it is possible to be humbly proud, I surely was that. I belonged! Belonged for time and eternity to the God of my Fathers, the God of Abram, Isaac and Jacob, because of the mediating death and Resurrection of the sinless Lamb of God, *Joshua Hamoschiach.*

No more did I fear my enemies. If I were arrested I knew it would be God's will that I should enter a situation to bring His comfort to others. Was I ready for such a task? I was no Paul, nor Peter. I'd only known my Master for minutes. Again biblical truths flooded my mind. "Have not I made the mouth? I shall be with you; I shall go before you. I shall give you to speak in that hour, what you should say. Only be strong and of a good courage. Heal the sick, cleanse the lepers, proclaim the good and acceptable year of the Lord."

That day I was truly emptied, an empty channel. If only I didn't choke it by selfish interests or foolish fears. "Pray without ceasing! Watch and pray that ye enter not into temptation!" There they were once more, the words from the Scriptures. My heart was lifted up almost continually. He remained close and dear and was always interested in all my doings. He listened to my regrets and His advice was always correct.

By the end of that day, Easter Monday, 1944, Sister Moony, having watched me curiously, asked why I seemed so pleased with myself.

What could I say? "Almighty God is really terrifically wonderful," I beamed. At this she frowned, peered into my face, then shrugged her shoulders, sighed and went on with her book.

Inwardly I repeated "terrific and wonderful." Yes, He was all that and much more, but we, His creations, were so far away from His will and His purpose for our individual lives. Furthermore, my people—their unnecessary suffering, the fear among young and old, the premature murderous death of all those millions, war, hatred. God was terrific and wonderful, but why not we His children? Were we His in name now? Had we, as a people, gone our own way, become introverts instead of listeners and His obedient followers?

Oh! All the world was in a muddle; all the world was full of turmoil; all the world! The world consists of people. *Individuals make or mar the world!*

Here I was, I could not do otherwise, I'd love to follow the Way of God mapped out by the Lord Jesus

Christ. It spelled love, truth, purity, freedom, joy, salvation and perfect assurance of a living eternity in Christ's presence.

"Don't fear what men do unto you, they can only kill the body but not the soul. Fear rather Him who can destroy both body and soul in hell" (*see* Matthew 10:28).

That was strong language, but He had said so, and His words are spirit and truth.

During the next few weeks I devoured all I could of both the Old and New Testaments. A new world lay before me, a life that was endless and a future that was secure, however much men interfered.

This gift of security came at just the right time. Mrs. Goody gently broke the news to me that I could not stay with them till the end of the war. It was too dangerous in such a small house to cope with two illegal persons. Ordering food for two and buying what was necessary for four people could easily arouse suspicions.

During the next few days events moved rapidly. We had visits from the courageous nursemaid of the manse and from Tantje. They brought news and equipment for false identification cards, fingerprints and passport photographs. My name, date of birth and address were false, while a real fingerprint and photograph ensured a semblance of reality.

While Uncle Bas was our key figure in the north, Uncle Henk was his counterpart in the south. He told me that I had one week to prepare myself for yet another long journey on the conveyor belt of human ingenuity. And, best news of all, I was to go for a night and a day to the manse!

Sister Moony's good-bye was as cool as had been her general attitude throughout my stay. But my joy at the thought of seeing my old haunts, of being able to speak with Aunt Jo about my Saviour and Master, made me bid her farewell graciously.

CHAPTER 15

It was pitch black when I left quietly by the front door, walking smartly away with a gentleman who passed our door at the appointed time and signal.

Two bicycles waited at the far end of the next street. When I was handed one I realized what was expected of me. Silently we cycled along the dark country road until we reached the manse. Once more I entered by that familiar back door, remembering a similar entry some nine months before.

Aunt Jo was as calm as usual and so was I. Her instructions were short, to the point and unemotional. Only at the end she added smilingly, "Remember, it is written: 'Lo I am with you alway, even unto the end of the world.' "

We had little to say after that. Aunt Jo had to face the rest of the war on her own. Uncle Bas faced arrest and possible death if he were caught; yet, occasionally, his tall lean figure would tap the secret code on the shutter windows and he could snatch a few minutes with his loving wife. He dared not see his son, for the boy was old enough to reveal that "Daddy has been home."

Tantje joined us and Aunt Jo played our favorite

hymns, while we sang or hummed along. His Presence was very close to us—so close I felt the need for prayer to see me through the unknown days ahead.

"Would you pray for me, Tantje, pray with me, before I go away?" I asked.

Her usual big grin disappeared and a scarlet flush transformed her face; I realized no one had ever asked her to pray for them before.

Reverently, she addressed our Master slowly and simply. She asked Him to let all of our plans work out smoothly, to restrain the enemy, and to watch over us. "Let all be still this night to let these people escape freely," she ended.

After the "amen," Aunt Jo told us that the time of my departure was at hand.

Our good-byes were short, and Nopje and I stepped out into the stormy, dark night. It was dry, but the lashing rain of the day had left the ground so soggy our boots were sucked repeatedly into slithery bogs. We struggled along the right side of the rails toward the station, until we saw a light and two people approaching us. We took shelter for a moment, then Nopje followed them—one was Domie!

Everything depended on the next five minutes. No fear must enter our hearts, yet mine was thumping and puffing in rhythm with that engine.

Nopje pressed my hand lovingly and firmly, then I walked on with Domie. He opened the door of the nearest carriage. We were in the "belly of the whale." It was the Urlaub train all right, packed with *wehrmacht* returning from leave, and going back to the front line—back to duty.

Roughly sliding open compartment doors, Domie shouted in German, *"Nirgends Platz? Schrecklich?"* ("No seats anywhere?") through car after car. Suddenly, he pushed me forward and exclaimed, *"Na Endlich! Aufwiedersehn und gute Reise!"* ("Well, goodbye, and a safe journey!") "Until Utrecht," he added softly in my ear. Then he committed me into the care of the Shepherd of our souls, turned and slammed the compartment door after him.

I moved slowly toward the only vacant seat, among seven sleepy soldiers. I excused myself in proper German; they all smiled sleepily, shifted their positions, and closed their eyes again. I settled myself comfortably among them and soon joined them in dreamland.

When the train eventually jerked to a halt, we all awakened almost at the same time. We were in Utrecht.

Calmly and slowly, I rose, stretched and rubbed my eyes. *"Aufwiedersehn, all Gute!"* ("Cheerio, all the best!") I said and slipped into the aisle, out the door and onto the platform milling with people. It was so exciting to mingle with ordinary people—men and women going to work—again!

"Gute Reise gehabt?" ("Did you have a good journey!") said a man's voice right at my elbow. It was the password, so I followed my companion onto another train, where he placed me in a special compartment. Two men smiled at me, and I smiled back. Contact had been established.

Toward evening we entered the most southern part of Holland. I'd never been here before. The countryside looked different from that at home. There were hills and valleys, quaint villages and far more churches. The passing stations were packed and the roads were amazingly busy, too; it looked like the evening rush hour. Our train did not stop at every station, but the compartment began to empty itself slowly. At last the two men and I were alone. The older man was around forty years of age and the younger one, introduced to me as his son Dirk, was about eighteen. After a friendly welcome they gave me a sandwich box containing slices of bread and cheese still juicy and fresh.

We left the train and mingled with the rush-hour crowd. Everything was timed perfectly. They took me to a lonely farm outside the city boundary where a delightful meal awaited us. I was allowed to wash and change my clothes. (Once properly laundered they would do for some other young girl.) My new outfit suited me remarkably well.

Uncle Henk and my hostess withdrew to discuss the

arrangements for the next twenty-four hours. Dirk and I discussed superficial matters including the ever pressing remarks about the weather.

When our seniors returned, we learned that their decision was to make use of the last dark night and deport me at once, after midnight. Here I was called Francisca officially, as my false identity card confirmed this now. My new name had become part of me; my age, occupation and address practically a reality. I lived and moved as Francisca Dobber.

I learned from my guides that while I was being conducted to safety, terrible things had happened to my fellow undergrounders. The mice had been caught, after being placed in selected families by people like *Oom* (Uncle) Henk, Dirk and Domie. Some traitors had smelled out the illegals and betrayed them for material gain. The mole, best friend of the mice, had guided and guarded their travels but he, too, had been caught.

He was stong and fit and had a chance of surviving, but the mice, especially the little one, couldn't stand up to it. Suddenly arrested, she was dragged to a prison in Amsterdam, then to a camp in Westerborg and from there. . . .

The worst was confirmed by a letter which reached Aunt Jo some time later:

> Friday afternoon, while standing on the station at W. I saw a long train passing which had come from the central camp at Westerborg. From one of the cattle trucks, three women, standing behind an open latch covered by barbed wire, called something to me. I could not get very near because the whole station was full with the enemy police force which kept people from getting closer. I knew these poor people wanted desperately to tell me something, then I made out your name and address. They wanted to greet you once more. I hereby pass this message on to you.
>
> Yours sincerely, Captain K.

But one had to go on. No more surrender could be tolerated from us since we had been saved so long and at so great a cost.

We arrived at a quiet little street and Oom Henk tapped his secret code message on the window. A door opened and we entered the dark house. Once fully sealed off, the lights went on in a small room, and we exchanged greetings in a whisper. A cup of tea was poured and, after eating, Oom Henk assured me that he would be back in a few days' time.

Quietly, my new housemother guided me to a room with a double bed. Her teen-age daughter was sleeping and I had just to slip in beside her. She knew I was expected and would meet me in the morning if I were awake before she left for work.

Having carefully attended to personal necessities, I stepped carefully into the "preheated" bed. Sheer exhaustion took over and soon I knew no more.

The sun was high in the sky when I opened my eyes. The space beside me was cold, indicating that my bedmate must have left long ago.

The room was barely furnished, with only necessities and a few cheap ornaments on a very battered chest of drawers. The bed had, well, not quite clean sheets, and this made me push the top sheet from my chin, but—I was safe!

The door opened slowly and quietly. "Are you awake?" my hostess inquired. "Here, put these slippers on if they fit. I've made a fresh pot of coffee for us both."

I did like that lady! Such a motherly, hearty and wholesome soul. She called me Francisca and I called her *Moeke* (Dutch nickname for Mother). Everyone was just Mum and Dad.

The day dragged along slowly; I helped with simple and quiet jobs. At last it was time for the evening meal. I met the teen-age daughter properly—a nice bright girl who had a little nervous twitch in her eye. Rather attractive, I thought.

As we chatted during the evening hour, I sensed she harbored a kind of sorrow for me. Here we were together, discussing subjects of equal interest to us both, yet living lives which were miles apart. The one had freedom, the other enforced captivity—one a life of planning, the other just a patient waiting. Hers was a life of sacrificial sharing, mine, of necessity, that of helpless recipient. There was just one factor which made me shudder with horror and fear—her hair was alive!

That night I invented an excuse and laid a towel on my part of the pillow, then casually wrapped it round my head. Jokingly, I told her that I felt it drafty at night.

Tomorrow would be the third day and Oom Henk would come to check if I had settled down and if Moeke wanted to keep me. I didn't mind the place, the people, the atmosphere, but I hated the creepy-crawlies so near me at night. Could I mention them to Oom Henk? One just couldn't hurt Moeke, yet she ought to know, for others would feel like me in days to come if nothing was done to exterminate them.

That night I lay awake for a long, long time, almost listening for conversation among the animal life. They must have declared a state of emergency, the decision being "either she goes or we go." They knew, but their owner didn't; she slept the sleep of the righteous!

Carefully I combed my hair next morning. Very carefully indeed! Somehow the enemy must have sensed my attitude. It seemed as if they found me entirely unworthy of invasion and permanent occupation. None had been eager to sample my island. I was still alone!

A delighted Francisca welcomed Oom Henk that afternoon. He asked if I'd settled in, and wanted to stay. I elaborated on Moeke's kindness, warmheartedness, the happy atmosphere, the good food. . . .

Once my stream of compliments was fully exhausted, he calmly inquired, "And what's on your mind, my dear?" You could not fool a man of his insight. Hesitantly I informed him that my bedmate had—lice!

There was deadly silence for what seemed a long, long time. He nodded understandingly and mumbled, "I see, I see." I too mumbled, "Sorry, sorry." I just didn't know what more to say. How silly to be fussy about lice, when millions faced cruelty and death!

Oom Henk looked serious yet his eyes and attitude did not seem to be influenced by my army of little creatures. Something was wrong somewhere! Point-blank I asked him where things had gone wrong.

"Fransje," he said with a deep sigh, "we have just beaten them! Word has come through that they have invaded the manse, searching for illegals. Thank God you had left. That one night back there evidently started new rumors. Only Aunt Jo, Tantje and the baby were in. As it was 10 o'clock when they arrived the wee fellow was sound asleep."

They had questioned Aunt Jo nonstop, I was told. She had played on their human emotions by telling them that she was expecting a baby, but they had used the unborn baby as a weapon to break her resistance.

No, she had not given us away. But they put her into the lorry to continue investigation, after a night in a cell at H.Q. They never gave the slightest indication where to take the little boy, so Tantje had rolled him in a blanket and deposited him with one of his "uncle farmers."

Before they drove Aunt Jo to the cells, they'd even searched the church across the road, but had found nothing.

Oom Henk agreed that for security reasons, my unhappiness in this home might prove an irritant. He would resettle me that very night, explaining somehow to Moeke that I was unsuitable for this particular home. Reasons were never referred to.

It was not quite a moonless night when Oom Henk and I set out once more on our flight. This time it was a short duration. We landed in a home at the other side of the cornfield—a staunch religious house, apparent to anyone entering. There were fonts for holy water at certain corners. Large and small crucifixes adorned the walls of the hall and bedrooms and my new Moeke wore a golden cross and chain around her neck. She was young and quite pretty. When she introduced her two children to me I stiffened with fear. The girl was just six and the boy had turned four. She realized my sudden fear and worry, and assured me that the children were all right; they would not speak, they understood that we had to be hidden, had to be protected by —them. They liked the idea and had promised not to speak about us.

Us? I was whisked upstairs, where I reached out eagerly for the outstretched hand of Mami, the assistant head of our kitchen staff in Amsterdam!

We had a glorious view from our window. The path among the cornfields was in direct view, and we often saw Oom Henk long before he appeared at our door. He came more often to this address, using it as a sort of H.Q. for the families in this area. He was one of many visitors frequenting this home, and was not, therefore, noticed as an odd man out.

The district struck me as a devoted religious community. Mami confirmed this and told me about the many religious festivals she had watched. Many processions had passed her window and priests were seen in their flowing robes, visiting the homes. Choirboys in angelic dress carried containers, swinging them from side to side or forwards and backwards, and every now and then she heard a bell.

I told her of the religious observances in my home up north and we compared notes. Both of us agreed that these people were devout Christians, yet they were different from the boys and Uncle Bas, Tantje, Nopje and all the Christians up north.

Mami and I enjoyed many a serious chat. She thought me silly, however, when I assured her that the Christians read our Bible and held our prophets in reverence. I told her about my discovery of Jesus Christ, the Jewish prophet, who claimed divinity and humanity in one.

She warned me not to meddle in such matters as the learned Jewish elders had known about this since the days of its origin. I ought to steer clear, she advised me, of false teachings and learn humbly everything about my own religion. "But this *is* our religion." I insisted, "the trouble is that our people don't know it, they have to be told, Mami, they have to."

When I urged her to consider Christ's claims and search for the truth for herself, she hit me with the statement that if this Jesus Christ were *really* still alive and if God *did* care, we would still be at home with our families instead of being imprisoned here.

"But the people did not *want* Him," I argued. "He *is* alive, but won't *force* Himself into people's lives. He wants to be *invited* to live within a human being. Then, and only then will He rule that life and others through it. It is because the majority of people from all nations do *not want* Him to rule over them that this present turmoil exists."

She shrugged her shoulders, then asked me point-blank, "Do you believe that He is still alive?" I assured her that I knew that for sure, as He now lived within my life, at the controls of my deepest level of reason and purpose and action.

"Well, Fransie," she sighed, "you are no longer a Jew. Such a faith makes you a Christian; you may as well leave your hiding place and mix among the Goyim."

"You really go too far, Mami; one doesn't stop being Jewish when the faith of one's forefathers has at long last materialized, and one feels that reality deep within one's being."

She thought differently and we spent the rest of that afternoon in deep thought. She was the first Jewish person with whom I had discussed this newfound faith, but I could not fathom why this faith was non-Jewish and made her almost shudder. It was more of a puzzle to me why non-Jewish people glorified in our past.

Truly the world was upside down in more ways than one!

CHAPTER 16

That same week I begged my foster parents to ask their minister to pay me a visit. My New Testament said that communion with Christ was essential, and I was now determined to request such communion and its blessing.

The poor priest was shocked. Was I a member of the Roman Catholic Church? he asked. When I replied in the negative, he asked which was my church. I tried to explain that I knew nothing of churches—all I wanted was to take communion, because it was the wish of Jesus Christ that we do this very often in His memory.

That day, a human being denied me this intimate ceremony. I could not believe it! Jesus said, "Whosoever will may come," and "Come unto me all ye that are heavy laden. . . ." No exceptions were made by Him.

I did not mention my conversation with the priest, or its effect on me, to my foster parents; they were kind and charming—why upset them about something over which they had no control? And although Mami must have heard my conversation, she said nothing and we continued to get on well together. She and I did not wear the coarse and practical underwear which was customary in this farming community, and it was my silk pair of pants that sent the six-year-old running into the kitchen one day.

"Mummy, the neighbors are wondering about the pink pants on the line. Who hung them out?"

It was only suspicion, yes, but we all realized Oom Henk must be summoned. I hugged and kissed my little saviour, then Oom Henk and I set out again. This time we spent the first night in Oom Henk's own home, which reminded me of the manse up north.

Next night we were on safari once more. Here, there, everywhere—in and out of homes or thickets, fields or offices. Thumping heart, panting breath—at times not daring to breathe—listening and sharpening the sense of hearing for the sound of danger.

Needless to say it was a shock to me when one night no one came to collect me from the house I'd occupied the previous night. Could it be true that I was to stay in this pleasant little prefab home of a real mining family? A miner who rose at 4 A.M.—an exciting experience.

Here it would really be tricky to hide. A miner's prefab cottage, with houses on this side and the opposite side of our street. It was simple: stay in the back bedroom all day and move to the children's room late at night once they were asleep. Here, too, I was told not to worry if the girls should see me. They were perfectly safe. Fancy, another lot of four- and six-year-old chatterboxes! This was a real spell of hiding, no exercises all day and none at night. There was just silence, complete silence and no company. Jo was busy with the usual household chores and Wiel was either down the mine or sound asleep in the room where I kept my constant vigil.

My summer in this happy Roman Catholic home carries only glad memories. The Lennsens were a truly devoted family, almost childlike in their faith and their religious observances. We were one in our faith in Christ and our desire to please and serve Him to the best of our ability, looking constantly for His help, strength and wisdom, where our own showed its limitations and insufficiency.

We all had hoped to celebrate the end of this war

together. United in our prefab we had many a daring plan for celebrations in street and the local community center. One can, therefore, imagine our horror and shock, when, without the slightest warning, the now seldom seen Oom Henk rang our doorbell. He looked at the still bright sky. "It seems it doesn't want to get dark tonight," he smiled. "You've got to get out of here right away, Frans," he said seriously, "someone has been talking."

Sadly, we parted company that night, we who had lived so happily as one family.

There were some more frog-like jumps before me night by night, till eventually, another foster home opened its doors. Here I was once more promoted to the attic. Not to avoid the child, for it was only a young baby, but Mary was worried about her own father. Both she and her husband had sought for months to find a way to alleviate the lives of the persecuted. The problem was how to fool her father who sympathized with the occupying forces. He could not be fooled; the secret simply had to remain closely guarded. They would accept a persecuted child or woman, and she would live among the low beams in their attic. A person who had no hope of life would not mind deprivation, they reasoned, and the organization would pay for the upkeep.

There I spent most of my time in true solitary confinement. Never before did I have such close fellowship with Him, the invisible Christ, whose existence people deny. Our acquaintance became strong, our friendship secure, my dependence on Him absolutely unshakable, a certainty which I have proved in every smallest detail till this very day.

With warm love He surrounded me in that bare attic. He gave me courage when the air-raid sirens sounded their fearful piercing tone. When others ran to the shelters, He stayed with me. His Holy Spirit, able to be everywhere at the same time, covered me with security. I knew myself loved, even when no human being considered my need. His cross became my symbol of ultimate victory. I wanted to possess one, just to hold it, to touch it, to finger its outline.

The potato knife was strong and sharp. With it, I shaped carefully two pieces of wood of the same width, which I found among the beams. Not able to join them with nails, having to avoid hammer blows, I pressed some tacks in the center and soon had fashioned a cross of my own. Pleased with my effort, I set out to paint it with shoe polish, and then rubbed it to a lovely shine. From then onwards, furniture polish enhanced its beauty! If you could see it today, no roughness in the wood would remind you of its origin.

For some days after I completed the cross, a general feeling of malaise invaded my body. I could not eat and developed a tremendous thirst. Then I started to cough and, within a few days, the cough was preceded by a whoop! Ridiculous—how could I a teen-ager, a nurse, have caught this childish infection in my solitary confinement? Yet, as both cough and whoop became worse, I knew I had to do something, lest someone hear me. That could cost us our safety and possibly our lives.

My landlady, Mary, was scared stiff, but she refused to call a doctor. After consultation with her husband, it was decided that I must make my way to the city on my own and find a doctor myself! I was to leave by the front door, pretending to be a visitor, turning to laugh and wave from the gate. Mary would give me the money to pay the doctor, and she would charge Oom Henk and the organization. Under no circumstances was I to divulge my host's name and address.

Next morning, at a quarter to ten, with a thumping heart and a happy bright face, I set out from my prison into the freedom of an entirely strange town. Waving gaily at the garden gate as instructed, I then closed it casually and left like a normal visitor.

Turning to the right, I walked firmly on and on, until I felt safe. I would find a doctor, I decided, but not as near as this; let the walk take me that little bit further "into freedom."

Soon I reached the doctors' area of the town. By

simply counting "one, two, three," the bell of the third house was decided upon. Bravely, I asked to see the doctor; the receptionist showed me into the waiting room. Oh, the horrible cough again and again. I wished he would hurry up. Would he object to the infection in his office? The bell . . . oh, he was a handsome youngish man in his early forties, dressed in an immaculate white coat.

"Good afternoon, Miss . . . ?" He inquired.

"Miss Dobber," I volunteered hurriedly.

Politely, he ushered me to a seat opposite his desk and straightway invited me to tell him what was wrong. No words were needed to oblige him of this subject, as a spasm of whoops and coughs supplied the answer.

Smilingly he raised his eyebrows, and equally smilingly I started my story once my breath had returned to normal. It did not take long to realize that my new stranger was perfectly safe. It was with a sense of great relief that I left house number three, a fully dated card with the course of injections to come in my pocket.

Almost sadly I trotted homewards, cheered only by the thought of the injections to come and the accompanying outings. My mind dwelt on the snatches of overheard conversation, the general feeling of expectancy which could be seen on many a face.

Could it really be true? Were the Americans outside Maastricht? Were the Allies advancing, or was it a wistful rumor? It just had to be true. Our people worried about the starvation in the cities, and if the situation became worse, we, too, would have to endure this hardship. Who then would be willing to help such a one as me?

My cough improved daily with the injections and undoubtedly the doses of fresh air during my outings aided the convalescing process. But Mary worried more and more about her father. "What if he wants to do some work in our attic, some modernizing?"

It was not difficult to sense just how scared she was, yet I just could not leave her. Oom Henk had not been to visit me for many weeks. He didn't know about the whooping cough, my outings and the certain knowledge that Mr. Metzger was a sympathizer with the occupation force. How could Oom Henk find another place for me at this stage? The atmosphere just vibrated with liberation and expectation.

The bombing raids increased as the troops approached the direct line to our town. Shell explosions were sharp and destructive. Frequently I held both hands over my ears to help deaden the crash which followed the eerie approaching impact. I gave sincere thanks every time my hosts returned from the shelter and I had survived another direct hit on my attic.

The last injection was due the day before my birthday, hence my inward celebration was observed that day with an overflow to the next. Never before had I felt an excitement comparable to that day. You could have believed we were free already. Dutch ladies boldly wore blue shirts, white blouses with red embroidered roses, or plain red bow ties. No one could accuse them of wearing the national colors; their explanation was that "all our other clothes have worn out and no new coupons have been available for a long, long time."

That day, August 29, 1944, I stretched my outing to its capacity, not even thinging about how worried Mary might be. I walked and walked along quiet country roads and through busy shopping areas. The windows were decorated with flowers and pictures, displaying only a little of the goods still available for sale. It all looked very attractive but rations allowed one just the smallest share.

True, it was summer, but to me it was more like spring, spring in the air, spring in the hearts of men and women, spring which even affected the little children. The advance was steady, the retreat of German troops, on the other hand, very noticeable.

Up north it was a different story. The month of August had spelled serious trouble for the manse. Once more the Germans had arrived to search for illegal food, such as corn and wheat which was kept in sacks upstairs. They "arrested" them and labeled each one for collection.

A few more weeks of peace had followed, very peaceful weeks indeed. Frighteningly peaceful! Then one day Nopje cycled up the front drive toward the house. The little fellow got his usual kiss at the gate, but Nopje's mind was elsewhere, Aunt Jo told me later. When Aunt Jo asked the fearful question, *the* question which mattered above all, Nopje nodded in affirmation. Yes, Domie had been arrested!

A young local policeman, after winning Domie's trust, had gathered as much secret information as possible, then betrayed him to the Gestapo. When the arrest was made, he allowed himself to be captured as well. Domie never knew therefore, who, along the line, had been unfaithful and led him and many others into the bottomless pit.

Nopje handed Aunt Jo a note which contained these words: "You may have heard by now that your husband has been arrested in Haarlem. He is being held in the main prison and is very brave under the circumstances, as he knows from where to draw strength. He wants you to know that he loves you dearly and that you too must be brave. Something is going to happen very soon. Be courageous!"

Later, more specific news became known. Domie had been arrested in the company of a Jewish person and two German officers who had deserted. During cross-examination they had done all in their power to make him mention names of the rescued. His nose had been broken and his eardrum as well. It was a miracle that his eyes were not damaged, as they set on him with rubber-loaded sticks.

The illegal movement did all they could to free Domie. A plan was laid to lift him from that prison on a Saturday. Everything was well prepared, and there was no reason to contemplate failure. But on the Friday he was suddenly transferred to the infamous Gestapo prison in Amsterdam. From there, no escape was possible. So that was what the writer had meant in that little note—"something is going to happen very soon." It was not to be. Poor, dear Domie now seemed to be imprisoned in iron shackles.

On that fateful day, Aunt Jo made arrangements to leave the manse, for she too, would be on the wanted list.

Mary, the mother of Jesus, set off on a donkey to flee from her oppressors and find shelter elsewhere for herself and the infant Jesus. That night, Aunt Jo set off on her bicycle into the unknown, the little fellow settled in his basket fixed to the handlebars, while a small case containing all her earthly possessions was attached to the back carrier.

Wearily and alone she cycled carefully many, many, miles, not knowing how to answer the constant questioning of her small son. No, she didn't know herself when they would return home. Nor did she know when he would go to bed. When darkness fell, she requested hospitality at the nearest manse. Thereafter it was a case of one manse this night, another one the next, avoiding too long a stay at any one welcoming home. Finally she reached Winschoten where she gave birth to her second son, Erik.

It was to be another six to eight weeks before it would be safe to go back to her own empty residence. During her absence, the Youth Organizations, under Tantje's expert direction, cleaned the whole building, making it liveable once more, and preparing it for the sad homecoming of their minister's wife and children.

As I stood at the edge of the pavement, crushed by other well-wishers, waving and cheering the slowly approaching American tanks, tears dripped unashamedly down my cheeks. Here I witnessed the liberation, freedom was mine, the nightmare was over, over forever but . . . no Uncle Bas to whom I could express my gratitude. No one close, no one who belonged to me and no one to whom I belonged, except Him, the Creator of the Universe.

We were free, but Holland itself was still tight in the grip of the enemy. This last winter was the worst one for the people of Holland and the north. It was the infamous hunger winter of 1944-45. People exchanged their gold and silver for potatoes and bread. The black market did a thriving trade. Some became rich overnight while others faced poverty and hunger for the first time in their lives.

That winter goes down in our history as the bleakest for centuries. Yet, here in Limburg, people began to live. We were free, happy and eager to breathe to the full.

Mary told me plainly that they could not possibly keep me any longer. They had not heard from the Organizaton, which, translated, meant "no cash is forthcoming." I took the hint and informed her that I would leave at the weekend.

On Wednesday I roamed the streets again. I possessed no money, not a cent, but there was gladness in my heart, and a gratitude to the countless dozens of people who had knowingly, or unknowingly, contributed to the preservation of my life.

Jesus said, "I have given you this as an example so that you may do as I have done. . . . Once you have realized these things, you will find your happiness in doing them" (John 13:15, 17 PHILLIPS).

I had many examples, coutless examples. I had seen Christ at work in people of different age groups, professions and social standing. They had but one thing in common: selfless devotion to the Christ, who had become my Master and Lord as well. Would I be able to serve Him in such selfless fashion in the service of my fellowmen?

"There is no greater love than this—that a man lays down his life for his friends" (John 15:13 PHILLIPS). That was what Domie, my Uncle Bas, has done for me. I would never be worthy of such a sacrifice. With Christ's inward help, I would try to live a life of love, giving and sharing all I had and all I was.

I had mused so deeply that I had not noticed that I had returned to the street and house where Mary lived. Hesitatingly, I stood there for a while, when a tap on my shoulder made me turn. There was Mrs. Heemskerk, our neighbor from across the street. "Coming for a chat in the garden?" Of course I would!

In reply to Moeke Heemskerk's gentle questioning, I

heard my own voice telling of my predicament, my hopes, my determination and plans for work.

At last Moeke asked in a quiet and warmhearted voice, "Would you not like to come and stay with us just for a little while, Fransje? Just to experience the feel of a normal home? I have three girls, one is your age, you would love it, Frans. Do as you like, but learn to live normally again."

Tears welled up in my eyes. I could not answer her at all. Here was my open door—but how would Mary feel about her neighbor? Then my material poverty brought me to my senses. I told Moeke that I had no money for my keep, that nothing had been heard from the Organization for a long time. Of course, I would look for work at once and give her all I could. She stopped my flow of words, assuring me that I would just be one of the family, sharing all they were able to afford. My next objection was the consent of her husband and children, who knew nothing of her decision. She dismissed all my fears in one sentence. "I don't need to ask them; all of us would love to have you in our midst. I am the mother, I know my family."

Thoroughly happy, I left that front garden and went straight to my attic in Mary's house. Going down on my knees where no one could see me, I gave humble thanks to Him who had continually watched over me.

After dinner I lay on my mattress quietly and thoughtfully, a pencil and paper clutched in my hands. Much had to be planned and essentials attended to. How could I begin to search for my parents and other relatives? Holland was still at war and heavily oppressed. No mail could reach the destination of our Red Cross H.Q. All the same I would make statements and have all details ready and in perfect order for legitimate inquiry, whenever that would be.

On Saturday I would move to the Heemskerks', and spend an official Sunday in a Christian home and take my first walk to a church, their church. I could hardly wait. If only Uncle Bas could know. How would he be spending his Sundays? I prayed: "Oh, Uncle Bas, may God Almighty be in these walls, be inside you, to strengthen you and soften all the hard blows by the example of His own endurance when under persecution."

One Sunday in Cell A 119 Domie, through the medium of a stump of a pencil and a piece of toilet paper, expressed his deepest feelings:

I knew that Thou dost always watch the humble
and those who wait for Thee,
Therefore I had this certainty,
I'd never be alone;
My broken heart be healed by Thee in time.

But I didn't know that Thou wouldst come
bowing deeply, entering this low door,
Witnessing a golden light astreaming through the window
transfiguring our shamble here with scented melody.

That rising reverently these walls would face Thee,
pronouncing a three-fold "Holy Your Majesty."
All the bare structure with folded hands would praise Thee
because of old and now. Thy ways are merciful.

And I? For bread and water I do give Thee praise
partake communion with all Thy Church which strays,
In here, Thy Name's uplifted by angels and poor me . . .
while all creation Thy works can't fail to see.

How possibly could I lose so soon
this unity with Thee my Lord,
Conversing here with Thee
when Thy will's mine and mine is Thine?

My folded hands just rested in Thy grip.
    My heart just beat by power from Thy lip.
My eyes just see the greatness of Thy might.
    When weak, Thy strength was always just in sight.

Then came the knock . . . such shock . . .
    when I was called for that last walk!
Within me all so calm. . . .
    Thy heav'nly music my eternal balm.

For one can go in peace when trusting in Thy Word
    raised hands in blessing, inward courage heard.
Since I belong to Thee in body and in soul
    Death is Life! I've reached my goal!

Bastian Johan Ader
(translated by Johanna-Ruth Dobschiner from the original)

Yes, he knew when Sundays came round. He encouraged his cell mates, wrote sermons on endless rolls of toilet paper and sent them, tightly rolled up, through cracks in the walls, to the adjoining cells. Once a teenage boy was informed that soon he would be executed with others of his "crime caliber." The young lad was frantic and became hysterical as the afternoon wore on. Every studded boot on that concrete corridor shook him to the core, tearing his nervous system rapidly to pieces.

Gently, Domie took over. He calmed the lad, as only he could do. He strengthened and assured him with the source of assurance from which he himself drew.

Domie used not only his Sundays, but all his days and nights to portray the hope of this world in Jesus Christ, the only Mediator and Saviour of mankind.

This Sunday *I* would enter a church building for the very first time—a great moment indeed. My heart and my mind would be crammed full with memories and thankfulness, with prayers and sincere pleadings, but, above all, with a certainty that the invisible God would approve of my first entry into His earthly temple.

With sincere thanks I said a casual cheerio to Mary and her husband, assuring them that I would visit them often. When I entered the Heemskerks' house I felt as if I were a long-lost relative returning home. I had arrived! Now in a position to assess my situation, I could think about the future; a job had to be found, most probably nursing.

On Saturday afternoon we were surprised by a visit from an American Sergeant Major—a kindly rather plump man. After he had sampled our cup of tea he stated his mission. Would we be able to billet one of his men—the divisional cook? The kitchen tent would be erected on the green across from the house, and his men would eat inside the adjoining marquee. He was looking for billets all around this district.

Once more it was Mother, encouraged by Father, who gave him her generous "yes." That selfsame night two new people slept in the Heemskerks' home, the liberator and the liberated. Bill and I became close friends; he and I, both far from home, had much in common.

On the first Sunday of our freedom, the village church was crowded with men, women, children and American soldiers. There were few dry eyes that morning. Tribute was paid to those lost in the fighting and to all bereaved. The prayers and singing were conducted in Dutch, and I followed every word, praising my Lord and theirs, and then I suddenly realized that He was actually *our* Lord.

Monday morning and duty called us all. Jeantje was out early and Father had left at the crack of dawn. Bill's divan was back to normal, his blankets neatly folded in a pile. The little one played with her dolls and Betty had left for school. After I had helped Mother with the dishes and the general housework, I, too, set off to attend to my business.

First of all, I went to the Red Cross and left my name and present address, should anyone be looking for me. They inquired about my family and relatives and I supplied all known details. My occupation? Well, I supposed I could call myself nurse. Where did I work? Well, nowhere just yet. Almost pleadingly they asked if I could not spare some weeks for their emergency hospital. I was as relieved as they were when we parted that morning. A job already!

Jubilant, I made for home and late lunch. Mother hugged me tightly. We danced around the room. A job! Now I would earn some money—earn it by working well and hard in the profession of my choice. Too good to be true!

The next few happy months made me feel young once more. I learned to laugh again, laugh out loud, a forbidden act during the past year. It was fun to mix with girls of my own age and to be teased by the orderlies in the hospital.

It was a real emergency hospital! We made do with a great deal of improvised material. Most beds were camp beds. The patients stayed with us as short a time as possible. When the treatment was completed, convalescence continued at home. There were the odd cases, patients who found themselves displaced because of the partial liberation, those who were wounded by stray shells or debris flying around. There were the orphaned children awaiting admission into some home. They, too, stayed with us simply awaiting a vacancy. The elderly were our main concern. They needed constant care and nursing but above all, love and understanding.

When I had attended the local church for almost six weeks I thought it was time for me to become a member. The minister, Mr. Furnee, agreed to see me by appointment. As it was the first time I had spoken to him personally he was rather startled by my request.

He explained I could not possibly join his church without *Catechisatie*, (confirmation classes) and without being questioned by the elders. I would gladly try to answer any questions, I assured him. He wanted to know where I had learned my lessons and who had been my teacher. Eagerly I told him that I'd read the New Testament over and over again and was almost sure I knew all Christ required of me. Christ had taught me Himself. "All right," he smiled. "Come on Friday night to the vestry. I'll try to contact the elders and ask them to come just a little earlier to meet you. It may be possible that you could join the church on Sunday, be baptized, make your public confession of faith, and be admitted to the Holy Communion Table, we'll see."

On Friday night I was surrounded by many elderly gentlemen in black suits and black ties. All managed to smile a little while shaking my hand. Utter silence reigned for some moments after each one had taken his seat. Then Mr. Furnee made his speech of introduction before asking me many questions. The atmosphere relaxed and others indicated that they, too, would like to ask some questions. I enjoyed my evening immensely and wished it could have continued a little longer.

By Saturday lunchtime I complained that Sunday would never come. Mother suggested I should rest a little and collect my thoughts with prayer.

As always, my thoughts traveled back sadly many, many miles into the unknown. Where were my parents? Did I have any? How would my people have looked on tomorrow's act of personal decision? Many condemn a baptized Jew as traitor, apostate, turning one's back on one's own folk. I determined to show my people that this was the most irresponsible statement anyone could make. In turning to Christ, a Jew becomes complete! Christ Jesus did not create a new road, He cleansed and revived the old. He and His disciples were my Jewish brothers among whom I felt perfectly at home. Granted, since these early days many Gentiles had flocked to His feet. People of different nations and nationalities had found their way to God through Christ, but that did not change the fact that He came "to the Jew first," although "also to the Gentile."

No, I had no qualms about my baptism tomorrow. I joyously looked forward to this high honor and privilege to confess Him openly as My Lord and My Master; God Almighty!

I presented myself in the vestry at ten minutes to ten.

The elders arrived one by one and shook hands solemnly, and then came the Reverend Furnee. Mr. Volbeda, the local butcher and Sunday-school superintendent, volunteered to accompany me to my pew, then we all bowed our heads while an elder asked the Almighty to strengthen the minister to speak His word to all those who wanted to hear.

The minister led the way down the aisle, followed by Mr. Volbeda and me, and the twenty-four elders. I was led to the front pew and seated next to Mrs. Furnee.

We all rose to sing Psalm 95, verses 1 to 6, remained standing to repeat the creed, and concluded by singing the doxology. My heart swelled as I repeated the words along with the others.

Silence settled on the congregation as the minister opened his Bible to Mark 10:46-52. When Jesus asked blind Bartimaeus, "What would you like *me* to do to you?" the blind man replied, "Lord, I want to see." And the Lord replied, "Go your way, your faith has healed you." And Bartimaeus received sight and followed Jesus.

I, too, had received sight. I, too, saw the world with different eyes. My heart motivations, my intentions, my aims were all new.

> Heaven above is softer blue,
> Earth around is sweeter green!
> Something lives in every hue
> Christless eyes have never seen;
> Birds with gladder songs o'er-flow,
> Flowers with deeper beauties shine,
> Since I know, as now I know,
> I am His, and He is mine.

An unforgettable sermon! When the organ had sounded the last note, I heard the minister call me by name, indicating that I should come forward. Humbly I knelt on the special stool provided for that purpose. Folding my hands and closing my eyes, I experienced a high and holy moment indeed. It seemed that God had come to place His hand upon me. A moment to be sealed in holy baptism. He was my Father, I had proved it so often, but now He seemed to assure me, "I will not leave you comfortless, I will come to you" (John 14:18). My earthly father was with me no longer. He, the Father of the fatherless, had come so that I would *always* have a father.

While kneeling there, I identified myself with Bartimaeus. "Lord, let me see, *always*." I was determined to receive all there was of the Holy Spirit of Christ. The minister's voice broke through my thoughts and intentions. "Johanna-Ruth Dobschiner, I baptize you in the Name of the Father, the Son and the Holy Spirit. Amen."

During the words "Father, Son and Holy Spirit" I felt the cold water touch my forehead in the shape of a cross. When I opened my eyes at last I noticed the minister beside me. His arms were outstretched above me in blessing while the congregation sang the blessing Numbers 6, verse 24 to 26. "The Lord bless thee, and keep thee: The Lord make His face shine upon thee, and be gracious unto thee: The Lord lift up his countenance upon thee, and give thee peace. Amen."

I too said "amen", rose and walked thankfully toward my seat. The water on my forehead was still wet; I could feel the everlasting mark which no one else would ever see. I had been marked! Back in my pew, I remained standing while making official profession of my faith. I answered all the questions with the "I do" of the ceremony.

On the last "I do" the congregation sang my favorite hymn. "Whatever the future may hold for me, I know that I walk in God's hand; therefore with courage I lift my eyes to all in the unknown land. Allow me to follow without all those whys, I'll know that your doings are good, teach me just to walk each day with calm serenity and faith." The second verse ran something like this: "Lord, I will praise your love at all times although my soul doesn't understand Thee continually. Blessed is he who dares to believe, even when the eye sees nothing worth trusting. If Thy ways seem dark, I shan't ask why, one day I shall see Thy plan and purpose in all its brilliance, the day when I reach Thy kingdom!"

Everyone settled back in their seats; hymnbooks and Bibles were shut. The minister then addressed me: "Johanna-Ruth, may I assure you that the church, as represented here, is thankful to be a witness to the fact that this morning you are joining her as a proper member.

"In her name do I congratulate you most heartily on this very special event in your life! We wish you most sincerely God's richest blessing. It will be difficult to put into words what must have gone on in your heart during the last few weeks and days and especially during this hour. This is something between you and Christ! It must be very much!

"What we do know is that a period of life lies behind you and a completely unknown future before. I don't dare to suggest that you start an entirely new life of faith. In your relationship to God you have always known yourself bound to the God of Abraham, Isaac and Jacob, who is the God and Father of our Lord Jesus Christ, who will guide you also in the future with His trusted, indestructible faithfulness!

"The new part for you is the fact that you are now privileged to believe in the full revelation of the God of your fathers: in His Son Jesus Christ! The new part for you is that God has revealed to you that Jesus is Messiah, the Christ! The Prophet, the Priest, the King for whom Abraham, Solomon, Isaiah longingly craved.

"And what must you do now with this newfound faith? You'll experience a marvelously rich blessing! For the Christian faith makes you glad, it comforts you and gives you strength in all circumstances. It gives you inward assurance that, thanks to Christ's suffering and His death, nothing will ever be able to separate you from God's love, and that all things will eventually work together for good.

"On the other hand you won't always find things easy in this newfound faith. Neither outwardly nor inwardly. Many of your former Jewish friends will be angry with you and look on you as a lost soul and a traitor! Others may even turn their backs on you and hate you! But these are only some of the outward difficulties. Inwardly you will be plagued by doubt and questions like, Haven't I done wrong after all; perhaps the old learned rabbis were right? Or, What do I feel of Christ's presence? I've lost it all, does He really still exist? And what will you do then?

"Take the Apostle Paul as an example. Paul, too, faced many battles after his surrender to Christ. How did he manage? How did he conquer? In Philippians 3:12-14 he said, 'Not as though I had already attained, either were already perfect: but I follow after, if that I may apprehend that for which also I am apprehended of Christ Jesus. . . . this one thing I do, forgetting those things which are behind, and reaching forth unto those things which are before, I press toward the mark for the prize of the high calling of God in Christ Jesus.'

"Because I am apprehended! That was his greatest certainty and assurance and that also will be your greatest certainty and assurance. The old church teaching regarding predestination does not exist to frighten us; on the contrary, it exists for our comfort in life and in death. The fact that you have come in faith to Jesus Christ as your only Mediator and Saviour is no human work, it is God's work! God's Holy Spirit has begun the Christian life of faith within you! Wherever God begins a good work, He also develops and completes it.

"The God of Abraham, Isaac and Jacob, the God and Father of our Lord Jesus Christ has given you, Johanna-Ruth, the same promise as He gave to Joshua when he entered the promised land. 'I will not leave you nor forsake you!' This God keeps His promises. He is The Way, The Truth and The Life. Hold on to that! Amen!"

We joined in singing another Dutch hymn to close this memorable service.

Quietly we left after the Benediction. To my ears, the bells pealed on and on for a much longer time than usual. Outside we stood in brilliant sunshine while many people nodded with smiling faces in my direction.

Some stopped to shake hands, others invited me to come and visit them anytime.

Happily, we made our way homeward. An atmosphere of festivity settled on the family and Bill brought some delicacies when he came off duty.

That evening I wanted to walk on my own. I wanted to think and taste the feeling of freedom to do what I liked. Just one week between today's impressive service and next week's Holy Communion. I had been happy during today's service, but I was scared of next week's —the Holy Communion between Christ and those who seek His coveted indwelling, to cleanse and purify one's life, to accept His death and forgiveness, to experience His patience and love. I traveled back down the road we had taken this morning, past the now silent church and on to my mining friends, the Lenssens. I knew they would rejoice with me, even though I had not joined their Roman Catholic church.

And rejoice they did! We sat about, recalling old war memories, and presently, someone asked about my job with the Red Cross. Regretfully, I told them the latest news, which I had just received on Friday. The need for emergency care had dwindled at last, and the hospital was reshuffling both staff and patients in order to provide proper nursing care and administrative reorganization. I was among the redundant. But, I assured them, Mother Heemskerk had taken only the minimum from my pay, and I had a good nest egg saved up.

Hesitantly, I asked Jo and Wiel if they knew of any jobs. With a broad grin, Wiel nodded. Oh yes, he knew of a job, but would I like it? Would it not be too heavy for me or too tiring? They needed a few more office cleaners at the coal mine. "Quite a modern place," he assured me. The only trouble was that I'd have to start at 4:30 A.M. I would not get transport from Treebeck Would I consider living with them once more? I was delighted, but had to tell Mother Heemskerk first. Furthermore, it could not be till the Monday after my first Holy Communion.

Meantime he agreed to make inquiries at the mine, and he would ask if I could travel in the miner's bus.

The Heemskerks heard about my new venture in between fits of laughter. Fransje down a coal mine! It was too funny for words. We planned a lovely holiday week together. I would meet many of their relatives, traveling by train, bus and tram, just as in the days of old.

The final crescendo, Sunday's Communion! The men's suits were almost black, and so were the ladies' hats. It really looked more like a funeral than a glad get-together to meet our Lord and Saviour in Communion. The pews were packed, just like last week at my own service. At the front, however, was a long table covered with a white tablecloth. Something was on that table, in the very center, but it was covered with a large napkin. I decided it was the bread and wine, just as on a Sabbath day at home.

The service began as usual, but the hymns were more solemn and about Communion. Quite soon, the minister took his place at the center of the table. Mrs. Furnee led me toward a seat and other people followed. The church officer stopped the people coming for the first sitting when all seats were occupied. Carefully I listened to all the minister had to say. Lifting the communion cup with the wine, he blessed it and explained that it remined us of Christ's blood which was shed for our sins. When he broke the bread, he said it was to remind us of Christ's body, broken for us for the remission of our sins.

The plate with bread cubes came my way. I watched the others. Each put a cube in his mouth and ate it. I could see them swallowing. I fumbled a bit with my cube and then I too put it gently in my mouth. I swallowed it and bowed my head. Thank You, Lord! Abide in me forever, I prayed.

We filed from the table, others took our place, and the minister repeated his statements for each new company. I heard it many times that morning and even today, whenever Communion time comes round, I experience the same depth of His presence as on that first Communion on Sunday, November 19, 1944.

Late that afternoon it was time to move and get settled once more at the Lenssens. I really hated leaving Mother and Father, for theirs had been my first real warmhearted home since freedom had come.

As I left, Mother, suppressing her tears, gave me an envelope and said, "Keep it, my dear, and read it in years to come. We won't forget you."

> Dear Fransje, I would like to give you a few words now that you leave our homely family circle: God will protect you!
>
> Dear Fransje, we all hope that it will go well with you on your life's road and that your future may contain much sunshine and give you back all that was once dear to you, but above all a warmhearted homelife. May God grant peace very soon and that everyone may come back home again.
>
> These are a few short lines, lovingly written by your foster mother, father, and your sisters, Jeantje, Betty and Fientje.

Of course I read it often. I read into it all the good wishes of the host of people all over the country whom I will probably never see again. I've kept their wishes, their photographs, their love and their prayers and will always remember them. To them I owe my life, my health, my soundness of mind, my hope when, at times, all seemed lost.

In memory I salute them all—men, women and children—from up in the north to the low south, each one did their part to create within me a truly thankful heart.

It was fun, great fun to go to work at 4 A.M. Each miner in that lorry, as soon as he was picked up, went straight back to sleep leaning on another's shoulders. When Wiel and I climbed up the high step and took our places, a sleepy grin could be seen here and there. I grinned almost the whole road to the coal mine. All kinds of funny thoughts crowded into my mind. If my parents or brothers could have seen me shuffling along the road among these great miners! But it was good pay and I needed every single penny to get back to Aunt Jo once the war was over in the north. To find out about Uncle Bas was the most important aim before me.

The lorry dropped me at the central building. I met a woman coming upstairs with a pail, mop, dusters and a chamois hanging out of her overall pocket. It seemed natural to ask her the way. "The boss is down there," she nodded, and asked the obvious question: "Are you new?"

"Very new," I assured her.

At last I reached the place, where the noise was a mingling of tin pails, splashing of water and a mixture of dialects.

Certain that I was on time, it startled me when the boss indicated in no uncertain tone of voice, "Check all your gear and return it immaculate at eight o'clock."

"Okay," I nodded seriously, as if I had been given the most responsible job in the secret service. As I turned to seek the unknown, she called after me, "Office number nine." "Right!" I replied.

Office nine was modern, roomy, and easy to dust and mop. When it came time to chamois the large high glass partitions, the women helped each other. Since my office adjoined number ten, the cleaner there held my ladder and I hers.

Long before eight o'clock I returned with my gear to the basement. The boss still looked as grim. With a forced smile I counted out my tools before her. "Thanks," she sniffed. "Will you be back in the morning?"

Amazed, I answered, "Sure I will." It seemed that many of the staff were casual workers, one day here, the next somewhere else. "Oh no, this place suits me fine, just fine! I'll be back."

Jo enjoyed every minute of my long drawn-out account, and we laughed heartily over our coffee and rolls, and then I was ordered to bed till lunchtime. I did enjoy stretching out after that morning's work, assuring myself that it was a well-deserved rest.

Once more I was able to save and pay my way as well. A grand feeling indeed!

CHAPTER 17

Those happy weeks at the coal mine offices were interrupted by shattering news from Aunt Jo in her own handwriting. The words leaped out at me:

Dear Fransje,

Yes, dear child, the rumors you have heard are really true. They have shot our dear Uncle Bas. And I just wish they had done the same to me. It happened on November 20, one day after your first Holy Communion in which you remembered how the Saviour gave His life for you. Now Uncle Bas has given his life for you, as well as others. Have a look and read what it says in John, chapter 15, verse 13. That's what they printed on the little cards which were distributed in Driebergen when Uncle Bas's body was taken there from Veenendaal where it had been buried illegally. Now it rests in the family grave.

That body of Uncle Bas! What wear and tear it had endured! At last it is at rest. But his burning spirit is alive. I believe that he is very close, inspiring me to continue his work. I really find in doing so my fulfillment in life. Bas-Janneke talks much about his daddy. Little Erik (his brother) was only sixteen days old when his father was called for his last walk. During that walk he folded a page in his hymnbook at hymn 139, verses 10 and 11, I suppose for us who were left behind. [A Dutch hymn which speaks about the Father's true care; that really nothing can happen to us which is not tolerated by Him. He has promised to be with us in all circumstances and situations, and see us through.]

They took him from prison in Amsterdam for something he knew nothing about. There had been an attempted assassination on a high-ranking German official in Veenendaal. First of all it had been decided that Veenendaal people would have to suffer. The Lord Mayor, however, pleaded for his townsfolk, so an agreement was reached to extradite six prisoners from Amsterdam in alphabetical order. Ader was the first. Some have never been identified, but Uncle Bas had his hymnbook with his name. his was found on his body.

If you can, and when you can, travel up north, my dear; we'll be able to talk about your future. And remember always that we are surrounded on all sides by the world of spiritual values. Much love from Aunt Jo.

Numb and cold, with my heart thumping heavily, I sat for a long, long time holding that letter. Uncle Bas dead, shot dead. Our Uncle Bas!

He died to secure my life in this world.

Christ died to secure it in the next.

Life here and life eternal by the shedding of blood.

"Greater love hath no man than this, that a man lays down his life for his friends."

Would I ever be capable of true love, selfless love which entails true sacrifice? "Lord make me worthy of such sacrifice, privileged to live at such cost—Domie and Christ." This was my prayers.

I just had to get up north. It was a long journey and I could travel only as fast as the troops, for not all of

Holland was liberated. From city to city I would make my way, mainly by troop transport, thumbing lifts. I could work wherever I liked and save all I was able to.

In each large city, I registered at the Red Cross Headquarters. Had my people been found? The reply was always the same: "Sorry, not yet, we will keep trying. Never lose hope."

At one particular Red Cross, I ran into a woman officer, who asked if I were interested in joining the U.S. Army Red Cross. Was I interested? I wanted nothing better than returning to my first love—nursing!

It was hectic work. We dealt with the repatriation of Polish soldiers, who had to be disinfected, reclothed, fed and provided with fresh sleeping quarters. Provided with high boots and DDT, we waded in and paid no attention to regular hours.

In our rare off hours, lady members of the staff were invited to socials, where we mingled with clean Polish and American soldiers. I couldn't dance, but I certainly did enjoy the orangeade, peanuts and chewing gum!

This assignment came to an end when there were no more soldiers to disinfect! But I was lucky, a lorry was leaving for the north on Friday, my officer friend told me. As long as I wore my uniform as a credit to the U.S. Forces I could keep it. When I had no further need of it I was asked to hand it in at any U.S. base.

On the journey I wore it proudly and well! Hadn't my hospital matron once told me, "Your uniform is the flag of your training school, wear it to our honor!"

The journey north developed into a pleasant holiday. The weather was perfect for the time of year. Motorways everywhere carried soldiers in all kinds of vehicles, and nationalities mingled freely. I met Scots, American Negroes, Canadians, English and, seeing that I had had hundreds of Polish soldiers all to myself for many weeks, only a handful from that nation.

Eventually I arrived in the capital of the north. My girl friend, Ida, now a staff nurse in the large Diaconess Hospital there, would surely be able to put me up for a short period.

It caused a pleasant commotion when a U.S. Army

Red Cross officer, speaking perfect Dutch, entered the hospital asking for Nurse Kroese.

A harassed Ida arrived at last. She had had to wait to see the matron to ask permission for me to stay in the hospital. There was no difficulty about that. I could stay, eat with the nurses in the dining room and have the freedom of the nurses' home.

On the first Saturday night, we went across the road to Ida's United Christian Fellowship—a social get-together of boys from different armed forces, nurses and local girls. The conversations were carried on in English, which was double-Dutch to me, but most of the other girls were anxious to try out their school English, and we all learned snatches of English phrases and slang. When it came to singing, we must have made quite a din, as we all joined in—the hymn sheets being duplicated in English and Dutch!

I began to feel conspicuous in my army uniform and with Matron's permission, I changed it for one of Ida's uniforms. And thus it was a "Dutch Diaconess" (European Christian Nursing Order), who set out for Domie's village.

As I walked the long road toward the village and the manse, passersby nodded and called out a polite hello to the strange nurse. My feet dragged as I neared the manse. This time I'd come alone; this time, there was no Uncle Bas to tap at the window and lead me in; this time, there was only Aunt Jo to meet me.

She opened the door, calling her usual "Come along in." But making conversation was hard going for both of us. I decided it would be best to ask as many questions as possible until we reached a common denominator. How was she keeping? Where were the children? How long had she been back in the manse? She, however, did not follow my lead but guided the conversation into other channels by stating that she would soon have to leave. A new minister would be coming to take over the parish.

We had come to a dead end. She was having to leave this trusted place. Domie was gone, but I lived to tell the tale.

I had so hoped to stay there for weeks, to have deep fellowship with her to whom I owed so much. Instead I announced that it was a great pity that I had to leave again first thing in the morning. There was a lot to be attended to and I was expected in Amsterdam. No objections were raised; it made me glad that I had acted thus. *Feingefuhlichkeit*, the Germans call it—the right attitude for the right occasion—tact!

The night was still as I lay in my familiar room. No one beside me in bed, no boys next door, no mice in the loft and—no one to fear. No sudden buzzes, no whispering voices, no one but Aunt Jo and myself, both with personal thoughts, unspoken statements.

It was true that Domie had died for such as me, but hadn't he been spurred on by deep convictions because he just couldn't do otherwise? The job had to be done and so few to do it!

Why had a man of his caliber been taken, withdrawn from the battlefront? Domie's view had been that no one really was ever withdrawn. Had Stephen, belonging to the first Christian fellowship, ever been withdrawn? What often can't be accomplished during our lifetime will find fullfillment when our body is at rest. He had reached more people since his death than during his lifetime. Even the one who shot him twice, through the head and the heart, had been touched to the core by Domie before the act was completed. He assured Aunt Jo that his life has never been the same.

Had it all been worth it, had he died for nothing?

That night my heart bled for Aunt Jo. She had to face life alone, still too bewildered to get her views into perspective and accept the fact. My presence had caused her more distress then the reunion was worth. It was a certainty that she would rise again, rise above her heartbreak and be father and mother to her boys as much as it lay within her power. Our heavenly Father would provide the wisdom and guidance needed for each step, of that I was sure.

It was an embarrassed, shy and very humble Francisca who left next morning. I felt as if I had left a slice of my life there, never to be touched again. Uncle Bas hadn't been there—the place lay cold and silent.

Ida wanted to know all that had happened and if I had enjoyed a happy time at the manse. Why hadn't I stayed a little longer when all the time in the world was mine?

I told her that Amsterdam was beckoning me. I had to visit all the old places, and especially the central office of the Board of Guardians. They were bound to have lists of camp inmates and their fate. Yes, I had to go to Amsterdam!

How was I to travel "home"? The U.S. Army uniform phase lay behind me and this diaconess uniform —well, I just wasn't ready for it. Ida parted gladly with one of her black gabardine coats and dark, plain dress, which we brightened with a white collar.

On a Monday morning I set off on the last lap. The last lap? That last lap was to continue from 1945 until the summer of 1953!

To arrive in a large capital, knowing no one and having nothing but one's memories, can be a very eerie experience.

Where had all the happiness gone? Why did no one smile? We had been liberated! Everyone went their own way. It was so cold here, although the sun shone brightly on my arrival. Were people more warmhearted in the south? Had the streets less people? Sheer imagination! Yet it must be true. There had been a war! Five long years! No city can survive without scratches. Scratches!

As I walked slowly toward the city center, it was hard to believe that reality lay before me. Incredible—I was now nineteen years old. I used to be so happy around these streets during my school days. Could it possibly have been a long bad nightmare? Had life to go on, just like this? But I had changed too, changed very much indeed. True, I was older, but more than that, I had become a dedicated person. These words rang triumphantly through my mind, as I trudged along:

The King of love my Shepherd is,
Whose goodness faileth never,
I nothing lack if I am His
And He is mine forever.

It could have been a tourist excursion. What should I view first? Our house! On the way I walked across the large square on which thousands of our boys, including my brothers, had been herded. Here they had to kneel in those cobbled stones for close to one hour. It was a sacred ground. Slowly and gently I walked backward and forward. Were there others in the crowd like me, on a pilgrimage? Looking around I saw no face whose expression betrayed a glimpse of its mission. What I did see was a monument—a sculpture in memory of our boys.

"Dear Werner and Manfred, I have no words, I shake my head, I mourn for you both and admire your courage. You have gone. You had no choice; you endured in your body the pangs of loneliness, hunger, torture and death. We shall meet again, boys, we *will* meet. No one can deprive us of that certainty."

Around the corner, the canal! Our canal! There was the turf barge, the plank from street to ship. It bobbed up and down as usual when another boat passed alongside. I walked more quickly. Here was my home. I stood long and silently, with all my memories before me. My eyes saw Father, Mother, the boys, Uncle Michael, Edith, Ruth.

"Hello, Miss Dobschiner, it's good to see you!" The son of the owner of the barge had come over the plank. He, too, looked up, and then at me, hesitant to ask the question. "No," I said, "I haven't heard anything yet, I'll let you know. It will take some time though." He just nodded and shook his head slowly.

"Who's up there?" I was eager to know. He explained that it was a poor family with several children, and the mother expecting another any day. The father was off work with T.B.

Here was our wooden staircase, clean and brightly

scrubbed by every tenant on the landing. How long I stood on the landing, dreaming, I do not know. Which door to knock on? My door? The living room? Or the main hall?

Hearing voices behind our living-room door I chose it determinedly. A very thin, tired-looking young man asked what he could do for me. When he heard my name, he pulled me inside and secured the door. While tactfully glancing around, I answered his eager questions about my parents and brothers. But I knew nothing. He hadn't given himself or me a chance to sit. Something seemed to press heavily on his mind. His wife, heavy with child, came down the kitchen steps toward us and raised her eyebrows questioningly.

"It's Miss Dobschiner herself," he informed her.

Mrs. Huigen suggested we sit down before we went any further. Went any further?

Interrupting each other, they told me a remarkable story, producing evidence within seconds. Spread out before me on that plain wooden table I recognized my father's and my mother's watches, her ring, earrings and a bracelet. From a kitchen towel he pulled a few sets of silver cutlery and my brother's silver pencil. There was an old coin which my mother had kept in memory of the twins' birth. There was also a silver replica of the Ten Commandment tables.

Astonished, I looked from one to the other. How on earth had they come by these?

They had been offered the flat when the Germans had confiscated all our earthly goods. The coal bunker had been left intact, but that was about all. Even the linoleum was stripped off the floors and not one curtain was left hanging.

"When the cold days came along, coal and turf were ordered and heaped on top of that already in the bunker. It lasted all winter and one was glad that a good summer had been forecast. The next winter, 1944-45, food and fuel were in very short supply and money even shorter," he added with a wry smile. "It was the toughest winter in my life. We literally scraped to keep going. We dug deeper and deeper into the coal your parents had to leave. We used it all, till the last lump and then—then we heard some rattling and found this cutlery. We were dumbfounded, and eagerly began to search for more, but nothing was visible—not till many weeks after, when cleaning our hall with a good stiff brush, we happened to press against the ventilation holes within the bunker door. Something fell into the dross and, when reaching down, I noticed a small ray of sunlight. It came through the now open ventilation hole. Carefully we unplugged each hole and found hard objects within all the papers. While the children were out playing, we completed the treasure hunt. So here you are, Miss Dobschiner: your parents cared for the future, it's all yours."

What could anyone say or do to repay such faithfulness? These poor people, who, like thousands of others, undoubtedly knew the pangs of hunger, had in their possession gold and silver which could have provided them much good food on the black market. A gold watch would have fetched a loaf or two of almost fresh bread—it was unbelievable.

It was with great humility that I accepted these well-known treasured items.

I promised to visit the Huigens often as long as I stayed in the city, and even afterwards I have, and always will, keep in touch.

CHAPTER 18

It was still early in the day, and inquiring for and finding the city's Red Cross H.Q. was an easy job. Something was strange about Amsterdam. It took me quite some time to realize just what that something was. It was the sight of empty and neglected houses throughout the city center. People were missing. Familiar faces one expected to see at this time of day were nowhere to be seen. They were gone! Shops were unopened or deserted, with dirty smashed windows, boarded up with wooden planks. Where were those merchants shouting aloud, advertising their wares while pushing a shaky barrow? And the children? Toddlers below school age? They had always played house around here. One used to push one's way along these pavements, waiting for a gap to press ahead. Now the narrow pavements were deserted.

At last I reached the H.Q. but their noncommittal answer sent me on my way in the same frame of mind in which I had entered those swing doors.

These hours in my city had to be digested. I set off toward the main Autobahn! Hilversum had been in my mind since the visit to the hospital up north where I had stayed with Ida. During several interviews with the matron, she had advised me to get in touch with their hospital near Amsterdam if I felt inclined to do so. It would be quite in order to mention her name and my stay in her hospital.

Soon I stood before the main gate of the Infirmary which was to be my home and training center for close to a year. At last I was accepted and permitted to peel countless pounds of potatoes in the hospital kitchen. Soon promotion was given: I could clean the large pots and pans, but the job had to be scrupulously done! Proudly I wore my black stockings and apron for this task. At last the big day came when the ward kitchen opened its door to me. Here I was closer to the people I wanted to nurse, the patients, but still I was not allowed to draw near or to touch.

At Christmas I performed my first official duty, watched by all the staff. Each novice took part in the lighting of the candles on the large Christmas tree. Our little group had been provided with one candle each. We found it beside our place at the table. After the minister had given his special address, our group came forward in alphabetical order. Before the tree we recited our well-learned text, in a loud, clear voice, then lit the candle and placed it in its holder.

Carefully I watched the other novices. When I rose I did as they had done, but recited my own text:

> Ho, every one that thirsteth, come ye to the waters, and ye that hath no money; come ye, buy, and eat; yea, come, buy wine and milk without money and without price. Wherefore do ye spend money for that which is not bread? and your labour for that which satisfieth not? hearken diligently unto me, and eat ye that which is good, and let your soul delight itself in fatness. Incline your ear, and come unto me: hear, and your soul shall live; and I will make an everlasting covenant with you. . . .
>
> Isaiah 55:1-3

Earlier in the day we had sung to the patients. Down

in the main vestibule a Diaconess played the organ, some Sisters had gathered there, while all the others spread themselves over the broad spiral staircase right to the top of the building. The ward doors were wide open and our carols resounded throughout the hospital. It was very impressive! Patients and staff voiced their delight with the bright beginning of this Christmas day.

A month later yet another ceremony interrupted the normal routine, if anything can be called normal in a hospital. We novices were "headed," not beheaded as some insisted on calling this important moment! To be "headed," we at last received our hat, our cap, to be precise. This made us proper nurses, having arrived, at last, at the stage of giving bedpans and cleaning the ward.

It was an official ceremony which all the staff were obliged to attend. The minister addressed us on the importance of our calling to this Christian hospital. All present then bowed their heads while we were sworn in by prayer.

The senior administrative staff filed past us and shook hands, while congratulations sounded all round. At last we were called forward, one by one, for the official capping. I felt like a knight, when I walked with uplifted head from the hall, with that cap pinned firmly on my head, and, under my arm, a prize book.

If Ida could have seen me that day, I thought. We were truly sisters, dressed alike, serving the same hospitals and the same Master. That weekend I wore my own outdoor uniform to church. I had become a Diaconess.

Our training was stringent, the discipline tough. It was for the good of the patients and the forming of our personality, we were told. We had our own rooms. When we were off duty, study, devotion and relaxation filled the day. Our free time was short, but the general atmosphere pleasant and happy. It did not worry us to serve long hours in the wards. We loved it, as we had given thought to the choice of profession.

Through my work I made many good friends. I visited homes and was invited to spend days in the Veluwa, the heather fields between the cities.

The salary, although not extravagant, allowed me to save a little. Britain still exercised its magnetic power and Scotland in particular.

Toward the close of my first year I made preparations to leave my country for good. When I left that hospital, many of the Sisters impressed on me, "Sister Hansje, never forget, once a Diaconess, always a Diaconess. The uniform is not needed to continue this service to mankind. Remember your consecration: *Ancilla Domini.*"

And so I left Hilversum, left my friends and my post, reminded that duty would be everywhere, at all times.

As usual, the first part of my journey took me back to Amsterdam. I made this a point of prime importance before the commencement of any other step toward—toward—what? I didn't know; the future was unknown. One step at a time: Amsterdam.

This time I traveled respectably, by train.

I decided to call on my old friend, Sonny Hakker. I made my way to the old house in Amsterdam South. The bell rang loud and clear. Quick steps and a voice —Moeke's voice. It was Moeke's indeed! In her usual quick way she opened the door wide. She gasped in astonishment, her eyes filled with tears while a delighted smile spread over her lovely face. Loudly she exclaimed:

"Han n n n s s s s je. . . .!"

We fell into each other's arms, embracing one another long and warmheartedly.

While drawing me into the living room she contined to shake her head, prononuncing only my name. Unashamedly wiping her tears, she asked me question upon question. Where had I been? Was there any news from my people? When did I come back? To each question I reciprocated with an inquiry about her and her family.

Mr. Hakker hadn't come back and neither had her only son. It grieved her to talk about these facts of stark reality. The loss of her only sister, even closer than a twin, had left her almost broken. But Sonny, the youngest daughter, was with her.

A persistent ring of the bell announced Sonny's arrival. Moeke pressed her finger over her lips for silence. No, I wouldn't say a word. "Sorry for all the noise," I heard her shout. "Could only press with my little finger, oh dear, I'm laden. I should have taken a shopping bag." Once Moeke and Sonny had disappeared to the kitchen, the clatter and bang indicated that her load had been dropped on the table. Discussion followed about prices and people, and Moeke's voice interrupting her daughter: "Come to the room, I've got a surprise."

"*Ha, blanus!*" she replied, as much as to say. "Who are you kidding?"

Briskly I heard her come toward the room where I was hidden, the door flew open and—"Han . . . n . . . n . . . n . . . sje!" she cried. "What a lovely surprise; you've come back. Good for you! What have you done with yourself? Your hair is a mess and where on earth did you pick up these 'fashionable' clothes?"

Typical of Sonny, her own sweet self! Oh, it was good to be there. Almost instinctively I knew they would ask me to stay.

Anyhow, I hoped so, for where else had I to go that night?

"Where are you living?" she continued. "Anywhere near?"

"Well," I began, "the truth is that I don't have an address as yet; I just arrived in town this morning intent on finding a job somewhere. Nursing or with children."

"Ah," they nodded, and then almost as with one breath, "why not stay here meanwhile?" They burst out laughing, and I could only join in and be thankful.

"Anyhow," Sonny continued, "never mind where you'll sleep; I'm starving so I'll set the table right now." She had taken over as usual. "We'll eat first and talk later. Do you still love Vienna sausages with mustard, Hansje?" Did I still love them? I hadn't tasted them since that day in the Weesperstreet, after leaving the Creche.

"I love anything," I assured her.

"Good!"

Systematically she pulled out the table leaves, arranged chairs, tablecloth, dishes, cutlery, all in a jiffy.

"You can relax a while and just watch and see if you still remember our delicacies.

The trolley squeaked through the open door, and Moeke, still with that happy grin on her face, pushed it in front of me.

I stretched my neck to admire, when Sonny decided: "Later."

One by one, glass and earthenware dishes arranged between bottles of sauces found their position on the white, starched tablecloth. There was fresh herring with little cubes of raw onions, the country's appetizer. The hot Viennas steamed in the center, surrounded by salami, potato salad, tomatoes, cucumbers, olives, peanut spread and an elegant cut-glass plate with slices of lemons for our tea.

Over this leisurely meal, we discussed our past, present and future. I learned that Sonny was to be married next month; her husband-to-be had also lost most of his family. They had found each other and love and had decided that life for them meant marriage. There and then I was invited to their wedding but . . . "not in that dress!" Sonny emphasized. With a hearty laugh Moeke assured me that we would find a "dream" for me. There was no time to wonder what that dream would be, as we moved to the next subject.

A job. The Jewish hospital could do with a great deal more staff. What about going there next morning?

It was my turn to enlighten them; it was a difficult task. I knew how they'd feel. It would have affected me in exactly the same way.

Seeing my hesitation, Sonny shuffled around on her chair impatiently, wanting to know if I wasn't fit enough yet. I could spend a little time with them; it would do me good.

It was time to speak, but how to begin?

"Moeke, Sonny, you may think I have done something terrible, but if you allow me to explain, you may understand and not judge me too harshly.

"I'll make it as short as I can," I said, "and then you can say just what you wish! You may think me rather odd or old-fashioned, Moeke, but although I am young, I do believe in God. Not because of all I've learned at *Cheder* (Jewish School), not even because of my strict religious upbringing, our family observances of diet laws and other religious practices. Not only because of the happy, harmonious family atmosphere it created, but because I've thought this out for myself, Sonny. Please bear with me as I try to explain. Although God is invisible I trusted Him, because His was the only Being one could rely on. Even when my family and all those other millions were killed after the most inhuman torture, even then I believed that a God was alive who would receive those suffering souls into some place of relief. Anyhow, I trusted He would. That was all. Then, when I was underground, a lot happened. I'll tell you someday in detail. What matters now is that you understand that it gave me plenty of time for reflective thinking. For quite some time I imagined that our invisible God would act, very suddenly perhaps, like the miracle of Jericho's wall, or the Tower of Babel, or the parting of the Red Sea and the drowning of the pursuers, the Egyptians. I lived happily in that expectation, but gradually realized that this was childish make-believe.

"After a while I read our *Tenach* (Bible) in Dutch. Only then did I become really acquainted with our history, our good and evil deeds. The promises we made over and over again to Almighty God and then broke. In short, it became plain to me that, although we are God's chosen race, Abraham's seed, Israelites by birthright, from God's point of view we are sinners and *Joum Hakipuriem* (the Day of Atonement) can't put us straight with God and make us acceptable to Him, for the next day we are just as bad again. We need daily cleansing and forgiveness, and that can't be accomplished, because we haven't got a temple anymore, where the stipulated sacrifices can be offered."

By this time both looked serious. I could almost detect a trace of real anger in Sonny's face, while Moeke questioned me impatiently. "What on earth are you trying to say? Have you started studying theology or something? You almost sound like a *Geschmad* (Apostate, a Jewish person baptized into the Christian faith)."

I nearly lost heart; it is difficult to explain a living conviction, when the listener looks at you with eyes of blind anger.

"There is something queer coming up," Sonny exclaimed, "but you may as well get it over and done with."

"Hans, *are* you a *Geschmad?*" Moeke asked bluntly.

"Don't call me *Geschmad,*" I begged, "before I've told you all I've done. It isn't as complicated or wicked as you may think. Yes, I have read the New Testament, that part of Holy Scripture which the Christians read, but not before I had thoroughly traced my way through Tenach. It was then I learned a lot that I had never heard at Cheder regarding the birth, life and death of one of our own prophets called Jesus of Nazareth.

"This Jesus was expected to come into this world by many, and He received a welcome when He was born. During His life He experienced their homage, and their reverence when He died. He was born a Jew, lived a Jew and died a Jew. His whole life's purpose was a task, a task from Almighty God, to act as a Mediator between God and man and finally to become all this, He accomplished a climax—obtainable by every human being who accepts Him as Master and Saviour—eternal life! Avoiding the terror and loneliness which death holds in its apparent finality, one can view this departing as rebirth into *life proper*. There is sorrow for those who have to be left behind. Sorrow in the separation for a while, but sorrow which is surrounded by an eager anticipation of the reunion there, where no death can part again."

"A beautiful sermon, Hansje," Sonny interrupted, "and so you believe all this—this—story."

"I believe, Sonny, that this Jesus is the Messiah promised to us throughout history. I believe that He lives and reigns and is willing by His *Ruach-Hakoudesh* (His Holy Spirit) to enter the lives of any human being who is willing to let Him in. I believe that He is God. God Almighty came to us in human form for a while, to explain to us what He is really like. Somehow, we, His people, have lost all contact with Him, have looked on Him more like a religious figurehead, rather than a living friend who is also King of the Universe. Because of His Godly, unexplained love, He thought of a way to show Himself as He really is, to create a way for the cleansing of our selfish sinful nature. He came as a human being, born into this world in an unbelievable way, as some of His actions may be unexplainable and unbelievable, but to those who accept Him and His ways *in faith,* they are power and salvation. He allowed evil to kill good and showed them that in this last instance evil is always the loser."

"All right, all right, you've said enough," both of them exclaimed. "We understand. You *are* a *Geschmad!*"

"I wish you wouldn't call me that," I begged once more. "I only accept in a most natural way what's been promised to us. There's nothing wrong with accepting the fulfillment of God's plan."

Quietly I added, "I know how you feel and think; you can't see any God who is interested in us with all this horror around us, with all the death and cruelty to innocent people. To me it's puzzling too, but then it is not God who hurts mankind, but we who hurt each other because of our sinful nature. The people who have done all this to us are not doing God's will. They obey the commandments of men. They do their superior's will, or their own, but *not God's will.* Don't let's blame God. He seeks continually to change men so that they will listen to Him and do His will. He approaches Jew and Gentile, rich and poor, old and young, black and white, and nationality and . . . He approached me.

I really want to do His will and obey Him and that's why I follow Jesus Christ. He enables me to lead a life which can be of use to Him among my fellowmen. How? I must leave that to Him. All I am privileged to do is to follow.

"So, *Geschmad* or no *Geschmad*, I'm the same Hansje as ever, just under new management, that's all!"

Moeke gave me a wry smile, but not a word from Sonny, only silence which seemed like eternity. She nibbled a biscuit. I wished I could drop into a hole in the floor. Moeke just sat there. At last Sonny rescued us all, including herself: "Come on 'Schmattie,' with all your beautiful butterflies, the dishes still have to be washed." Silently, we cleared the table, tidied the room, went into the kitchen and washed the tea dishes.

"I'm sorry if I've spoiled your evening," I ventured. "Don't be too upset, I know it's been a shock to you, but in time you will realize that this doesn't change a person for the worse, or make them deny their birth and upbringing. I'm proud of it, every bit of it.

"Hmm, we'll see. Let's get cleared up for the evening," was the only answer.

The kitchen was immaculate in no time, due to six willing hands. Sonny warmed up: the cooling effect of our discourse set aside, she made an attempt to create a worthwhile subject for the evening.

We had a harmonious time exchanging news of friends and relations. We grew closer once more, closer in our loss and closer in our aspirations for the future.

They were genuinely interested to see me settled, earning my living and making new friends with a view to a happy and successful marriage. True to tradition, they insisted on filling the role of my parents and creating a situation for matrimony. We had many a hearty laugh. Money didn't stop them from playing a make-believe game. "To your forthcoming engagement, with love from Moeke and Sonny." This pretty card was attached to a large bunch of dark red roses!

During the weekend I met Sonny's fiance—a handsome young man, slightly older than herself, and evidently deeply in love. I could see he had been told about my doings and that he took the matter very seriously, showing his disgust.

For the time being I slept in Moeke's bed. She had offered it to me, and she herself slept with her daughter on the large lits-jumeaux. These Dutch beds were my delight. The complete made-up bed, kept in place by three rubber straps, could be folded right up against the wall, underneath a modern bookshelf. Curtains were drawn across, and it looked like a streamlined wall fixture. As her future son-in-law was the manufacturer of the beds, Moeke had extra fittings added. This particular bed had a smart bookcase with sliding glass doors right along its shelf. On each side of the curtains, Moeke had planned special fitted cupboards, one for hanging suits and dresses, the other with pull-out drawers for linen and underwear. Once Sonny was married, the young couple would stay with Moeke and she would have to go back to her own bed as Sonny and her husband would move into the large bedroom with the lits-jumeaux.

I wondered where I would go after the wedding, but sensing my apprehension regarding the future, Moeke assured me that the young couple would not mind my presence. My primary concern was work—where I could eat, live and spend my off-duty hours. Only sleeping accommodation was of immediate concern.

Sonny had been able to interest me in the nearby orphanage. "It's a large modern building—a Christian place, too," she added slyly.

To the superintendent it was as if "I'd been sent"! They were one lady short in the boys' section which consisted of twelve- to fourteen-year-olds. When could I start?

"Tomorrow," I announced bravely. At home we toasted this quick success.

My section had twenty-two boys. Corrie and I managed all the work between us once our gang were off to school. Some came home for dinner, others descended as ravenous wolves on their meal at night. We mended torn trousers, socks, and worn jumpers; we played games during rainy weekends and took them to the country on public holidays. We humored quarrels and listened to their difficulties. In short, we were substitute parents and I loved my work.

If I could have settled down again, then this orphanage would have been a devoted task to accept. But there was a restlessness within me, and I realized the truth of the saying, "The heart is restless until it finds its rest in Thee." "If only," I thought, "I could be in the way of the Lord, know it, and follow it, my restlessness would cease." I was determined to search and pursue His will—then and only then would this striving end.

"Teach me thy way, oh Lord," was my prayer as well as the Psalmist's. Having asked for guidance I left it at that and continued my daily work in the orphanage. On Sundays I made my way to the Begijnehofje in the center of Amsterdam, where the Church of Scotland held weekly services in English. The minister came all the way from Scotland, and the worshipers consisted of tourists, students, schoolchildren and British people living in Amsterdam. I loved to worship there. I learned new words in a strange and beautiful language. Up till that time my vocabulary had consisted only of a phrase frequently overheard from American soldiers, "It's raining cats and dogs."

Although I could not follow the service the atmosphere was charged with the presence of the living Christ. Him, I was able to adore from the depth of my being. The language barrier didn't exist. On the contrary, I began to learn a new language. Following the lessons in my Dutch Bible, I carefully listened to the English text. It was fun. Soon I boasted that I could speak a little English when sentences flowed from my tongue. People must have been very polite when they did not laugh at my "Art thou hungry" and "I thank thee" to a child. It wasn't till much later that the phraseology sorted itself out. During the singing of the hymns I got hold of the pronunciation, but the general benefit lay in the feel of the language and the longing to see Scotland one day.

In the Begijnehofje, this longing was conceived. But how, how was I ever to get so far with no language, no money, no prospects? Yet, just nine months later, I arrived at the Central Station, Glasgow, Scotland.

During those nine months I had to travel another long, long road, a road which took me from home to home, from country to city, from village to town—a zigzag of a journey, aiming all the time for Scotland. Once more I had to meet dozens of new people, had to tell my story over and over again, yet in the framework of these simple accounts I decided to cross the border.

CHAPTER 19

My first and last Christmas in the city of my youth was celebrated in Moeke's cellar, with other Jewish teenagers. She and Sonny were fast asleep, but they had given permission to let me have my friends there. "After all, it's your home," they had emphasized.

There were seven of us who lived in Jewish homes; yet all had experienced the presence of the living Christ, and were drawn together by a desire to honor Him very specially, because our people had denied His living existence.

At intervals, a tap on the gutter window announced the arrival of yet another believer!

Since Sonny's wedding, I had taken up residence in the cellar below Moeke's bedroom. I loved the privacy of this place in the security of a home where true love was shared. Did they worry about my presence down there? I assured them I would not want to exchange it for the finest villa in the world.

Each night after duty in the orphanage, I would lift the hatch and descend to my own private domain. Just now it was decorated like a garden party in midwinter. All boxes and crates had been pushed to one side and covered with gaily printed materials, old curtains and rugs. My bed had a special, clean counterpane and Moeke almost buried me with gifts of fruit, chocolates and sweets.

Our number was complete by 11 P.M. and we made final arrangements for our departure to the midnight service. My guests informed me that it was freezing; they had all come supplied with woollen socks to pull over their shoes. I had no socks, yet when we were ready to leave a pair lay right across the inside front door. "For Hansje, from Moeke with love. Be careful!"

The sky was alive with stars, the air cutting our ears with its iciness, our hearts just thrilling with happiness and expectation. This was the night in which our Saviour's birth would be commemorated, our Saviour. Words can never express what a soul experiences to feel part of such union, to belong to such company, to know yourself a beneficiary of such divine security.

One of the boys in our group wrote and composed a hymn for this night:

> Royal child,
> with a crown
> Brilliant is Thy world renown. . . .

He sang it quietly while we made our way to church. We avoided the pavement, walking along the grassy footpath in the center of this large boulevard, and thus we were able to join in his hymn of adoration. We sang it over and over again—a group of young disciples as in days gone by. Yet none of our group was a *secret* believer. On the contrary, a fierce and determined flame burned at all times on the altar of each heart. We were ready to testify of Him to whom we belonged. Our testimony was a glad, definite affirmation of the privilege a disciple of Christ may enjoy. We knew ourselves called, chosen, loved and guided. Each with our separate background; each with our separate disposition and character; each with our different job and training; our aim was a common desire to love and serve Almighty God, who, as the Babe of Bethlehem, chose to enter the realm of humanity for a while.

The midnight service was impressive. We worshiped there, but far greater was the worship during our journey back to my cellar. No words were exchanged; no hymns sung; many of us held hands and our heads high: The King of Glory within had been honored!

When I opened my door, I could scarcely keep my tears back. What a spread met our eyes! Moeke must have read Matthew's Gospel, chapter 25 verses 31-40. Was she a secret believer? This is something between her and her Lord, but oh, how very kind. Thermos flasks with hot chocolate, nuts, cakes, biscuits, were a complete welcome for the cold troop of Hebrew Christians.

Around 3:30 A.M. we were eager to leave again. Local carol singers from the Salvation Army had invited us to join their company. It was a good opportunity to air our views in music and song. To forget our underground silence and sing at the top of our voices, "Glory to the newborn King; born, the King of Israel!"

At seven the whole group was entertained in the local Army hall. We remained together till the commencement of the early morning Christmas service where we listened to children's choirs, each taking part to honor Him to whom all honor is due.

During Hanukkah the little lights of liberty had burned brightly upstairs, but at Christmas the big light of love shone brilliantly through the dense walls of my cellar, and right into our hearts!

There was only a week to spare and then a brand-new year to make or mar. Nineteen forty-seven was waiting to receive mankind. The New Year was full of plans. Britain was still high on the list of my desires. Scotland, especially, exerted a strange drawing power. It was to be my "heavenly Jerusalem" on earth! Had I reason to place such high expectations on any country of which I had no previous knowledge? None whatsoever! Was this the way of God's invisible guidance? I was compelled to accept this as the only possible explanation.

Once my entire attention was turned toward the

country of my adoption, all other preparation proceeded without the slightest hitch. Moeke allowed me to save hard, adding here and there a little extra for the journey. I worked extra hours at the orphanage to make that extra penny. Still more was needed. At last I sold the family silver, the cutlery, the candlesticks and some ceremonial articles, which I would never use again.

A new life was beckoning. My father's only surviving brother lived in London and I longed to see him and look after him. He, too, had lost all his close family. Could we build up a new life together, looking after each other as our families would have wished? Would he be willing to accept me, a "Geschmad"? Would he be as understanding as Sonny and Moeke had been? It could be that my travels were not over yet, even if I found him.

I left little and prepared to take just as little with me. Christ had assured me that He would see me through. Nothing would be lacking, but always and under all circumstances my aim was, "seek ye first the Kingdom of God." He will do the rest, promised in His words recorded in Mark 10:29,30.

Countless farewell parties were behind me, but the last and most important one was still to take place at Moeke's house! It was a table fit for a queen. Sonny's wedding silver was out, also her best china; complicated and tasty dishes were prepared; bottles of wine, soda and the inevitable nuts and salty biscuits of all kinds were served. Was this a farewell from people who shunned, hated and despised your faith in the apostate, the false prophet? Those presents, good wishes and warmhearted love—were those gifts from cold indifference?

The Almighty has to bear constantly with our false and incorrect judgment of one another, and He advised Samuel, and also us, to leave judging to Him who knows best! "For man looketh on the outward appearance, but the Lord looketh on the heart" (1 Samuel 16:7)

When Sonny, Moeke and I arrived at the station I was flabbergasted to see the many friends who had come to say good-bye—teenagers, Hebrew Christians, old and young. Those I had dined with on Sundays after Church: those I had sung with on Saturdays around the organ; my boys from the orphanage, and Corrie with her fiance. It was my day.

Although all immigration papers had been completed and in my pocket for the past few weeks, the act had still to be accomplished. I was leaving my country, my friends, my memories. What did I take with me? My little black case, a larger one too, plus a bundle of hopes, faith and many worthwhile lessons learned.

Where I went, of one thing I was certain: What I was leaving I would find again, for Christ's ambassadors are scattered throughout the world. A Christian just can't be lonely, can't be alone, can't exist on his own. A Christian, by the very nature of his creation, must have fellowship with others. "Bear ye one another's burdens, and so fulfil the law of Christ" (Galatians 6:2).

What I could no longer give in Holland I would give elsewhere. The same sun, moon and stars which I had observed through the skylight of many a Dutch attic would shine in the country of my adoption. The heavens envelop us wherever we roam. Over us all reigns the same Creator. All countries and people of every class are alike before Him. He indwells all who invite Him to do so.

Where is the old, and where is the new? All will be alike. People with joys, sorrows, hopes and fears.

People who dare, those who don't care.
Some who do try, others just lie.
Few who are sorry, many never worry.
The gentle and humble
And those who must grumble,
Proud and unbending,
One finds them pretending
In countries throughout this whole world.

Then why mourn these partings,
Tomorrow you'll be starting
To meet the same over again.
Does language deceive you,
The heart will believe you
Certifying: Mankind is alike.

There was little to say as I stood at the window of the compartment, just the usual "Take care of yourself" and my constant repetition of "Thanks for all you've been, all you've done." Already I carried many little keepsakes and others were handed through the window. Someone insisted on the last taste of a Dutch delicacy: fresh herring with raw onions! A memorable farewell when I kissed each one good-bye with the penetrating smell of raw onions!

All too quickly the whistle sounded. I waved and waved till the train swung round the bend.

"Holland myn Holland ik vind je zo mooi" (Holland my Holland how beautiful thou art). This school song rang through my mind, while the wheels beat the rhythm on the track.

I felt grown-up all of a sudden. This time I was emigrating all on my own, seeking the new. I was creating a new life, in a new environment, with a new language and new friends. "Behold, I have set before thee an open door, and no man can shut it . . ." became the peg on which I dared to hang my young life.

"Lo, I am with you always." Countless promises like these from God Almighty hit my mind like laden arrows. Yes, I was brave with the good Shepherd beside me. Thy rod and Thy staff shall comfort me. Though I walk through the valley of the shadow of death *Thou* hast been with me and always will be with me I believe firmly, Lord, that goodness and mercy shall follow me all the days of my life and then. . . . Then I shall dwell in the house of the Lord forever.

Don't dream, Hansje, it's almost Rotterdam. There would be others waiting to shake my hand and kiss me farewell. Look out for Rotterdam—two more stations.

There they were: the whole family Ornstein, their neighbors, friends and the inevitable cup of coffee through the compartment window, a roll with cheese and one with tomato. I'd eat it later. The whistle—"Cherrio, cheerio, God bless you all, each one, cheerio!"

Hook van Holland won't be long now, get your two cases down, Hans! The trains drove right to the quay-side. What a large ship! Like a child, I could hardly wait to board it. There were formalities to comply with, customs regulations, forms to fill in, questions to be answered. At last I climbed up the gangway, looked for a space and rested my arms squarely on the railing, staring down into the muddy water.

Don't, Hansje, I urged myself, up, up, up! "I will lift up mine eyes unto the hills . . ." (Psalm 121:1). The hills—Scotland!

A free agent, I walked with uplifted head to a seat on the deck. There, lazing in a chair, I reflected on those years gone by.

It was one long severe thunderstorm—frightening and very dangerous at times! The rumbling thunder of threat and rumor was heard continually, then the crashing thuds coming nearer and nearer.. Would the lightning strike this night? The flashes hit right, left and center, then suddenly hit us as well, burning all that was near and dear. Still the storm continued—frightening, rumbling, striking all over this and other continents.

But even thunderstorms hitting continents, nations, countries, cities, villages and homes, must pass! Of course, they leave devastation, destruction and death.

A thunderstorm raged when the King of this universe experienced the act of dying for us.

Whenever electric storms hit your home or family life, look at the storm which shook Calvary. Allow it to be the yardstick for the circumstances confronting your storm.

The sky will clear; you will experience the deathly silence of loneliness, of despair, hopelessness, indifference to continuing in this struggle for life and then—after that silence, we shall come to see colors again, a rainbow through the rain! It beckons us to continue to lift up our heads, to look at that miracle of nature, that promise of Almighty God in Genesis 9:13-16. Presently the sun will shine again for you, too.

Calvary, storm, rainbow and then—brilliant sunshine! Resurrection! Also for you!

Believe it! Look for it! Lift up your heart, lift it up away from the base and destructive rumbling of doubt and fear.

Hold up your heart, mind, emotions, head and eyes. Up, up, there you will detect color again, brilliance, and promises with certainty of fulfillment.

While the wounds inflicted by the lightning still hurt and burn and undoubtedly will leave their scars forever, your general health will be bathed by the warmth and radiation of God's sun of love. You will tan and recover, stronger to determine your attitude for future storms.

You, too, will join the millions who quietly, humbly but very sincerely dare to utter:

". . . we know that all things work together for good to them that love God, to them who are the called according to his purpose" (Romans 8:28).

The ship had reached mid-channel. Surrounded by water and sky, I mused on the fundamental barrenness of material possessions. I saw no land, no human dwellings. I knew nothing had been left behind and nothing awaited my arrival.

An undying soul addressed Him whose twenty-four-hour service has one, and one aim only, to select willing souls to *live*.

"Praise, my soul, the King of heaven."

King of heaven, Father of mankind. My Father, my King. In this royal relationship, no poverty or death can sting.

Be persuaded when you hear His voice:

"Come unto me, all ye that labour and are heavy laden, and I will give you rest. Take my yoke upon you, and learn of me . . . and ye shall find rest unto your souls" (Matthew 11:29).

When you have closed this book, be certain that you, too, are selected to live. Never doubt it. Amidst thunderstorms, repeat it often. Repeat it when you are lost in a maze of worry and fear. Repeat it when you are baffled by life's problems with its avalanche of daily, petty strains.

You are selected to live, to give, to share, to affirm that Christ Jesus came into this world to instill new life into this artificially breathing world by living according to God's will and enabling you to do the same.

Selected to live, an undying life.
Selected to live an attached life, to its source.
Selected to live under Royal command.
Selected to live in service for others.
Selected to live!
Go forth and give. . . .
LIVE!

Please join me now in reverent silence,
Salute deep within you those who are gone.
Like me, you'll be baffled and won't know the answer
What really in mankind has gone wrong?

We don't know the answer; pretend we don't!
The wicked, they acted—we passive, permitted;
No mad demonstrations, not anywhere!
Individuals objected. The church was asleeping
And murders continued wholesale.

Prompted to bow our heads in silence,
We contemplate our united guilt.
Yet while we ask for wisdom, action,
Ne'er tolerate such crime again!'. . . . . .
Throughout the world, men, women and children
Beg us to notice their plight and pain.

Millions still suffer, they always will
While we are comfy, secure.
Not ours, but Christ's love must conquer that evil
In your labor of love for . . . ONE life.